SocialCorp

Social Media Goes Corporate

JOEL POSTMAN

New
Riders

SocialCorp: Social Media Goes Corporate
Joel Postman

New Riders
1249 Eighth Street
Berkeley, CA 94710
510/524-2178
510/524-2221 (fax)

Find us on the web at: www.newriders.com
To report errors, please send a note to errata@peachpit.com

New Riders is an imprint of Peachpit, a division of Pearson Education.

Development Editor: Robyn G. Thomas
Project Editor: Nancy Peterson
Production Editor: Cory Borman
Copyeditor: Darren Meiss
Compositor: Danielle Foster
Indexer: Karin Arrigoni
Cover design: Ryan Scheife
Interior design: Danielle Foster

ISBN-13 978-0-321-58008-5
ISBN-10 0-321-58008-7

9 8 7 6 5 4 3 2 1

Printed and bound in the United States of America

There is much talk about the "online conversation" but this has become a moving target because of new media publishing technologies such as Twitter, Friendfeed, and Seesmic. This fragmentation of media requires attention, and it takes a person such as Joel Postman to help put all these techniques and technologies into perspective. I've been saying for several years now that every company is now a media company, and every company needs to master the new media technologies at our disposal. Joel can help large and small corporations use the appropriate approaches because of his experience in journalism, corporate PR, and social media.

Tom Foremski, Silicon Valley Watcher

SocialCorp: Social Media Goes Corporate is a must read for any corporate communications professional. It also serves as an invaluable scale for balancing business objectives, corporate responsibility to stakeholders, and customer and influencer engagement. Joel Postman is a long time veteran of strategic communications and a proven expert in the socialization of marketing communications. His guidance will ensure that your company will not only stay on track with critical day-to-day marketing communications, but also increase brand visibility, resonance, and loyalty through direct participation in the online communities that expand your business opportunities.

Brian Solis, Principal of FutureWorks PR,
author, and blogger at PR 2.0

For Mom and Dad. And for Nini, Nathan, and Minna. I love you guys.

Thanks for your encouragement, and your patience, and for keeping me ever mindful, "no electronic devices at the table."

Acknowledgments

I'd like to thank the awesome SocialCorp interns, Bukola Ekundayo (who did extensive research and editing on Chapter 5, "Using Social Media to Reach the Right People"), Victoria Fennell, @Ghennipher, Clara Kuo, and @thegirlriot for indispensible help with everything from case studies, to managing the SocialCorp wiki, to doing research and editing. Thanks also to @epodz, Ian Griffin, and @vruz. Special thanks to the good people at PBwiki (official wiki of SocialCorp); Todd Hoskins of Networked Insights for his kind permission to borrow several questions from his company's "Readiness Assessment Tool" for inclusion in the SocialCorp Readiness Quiz; and to Richard Kastelein of Expathos for his kind permission to reproduce portions of his company's "Social Media Dictionary" for use in the glossary of this book.

Finally, there are hundreds of people who have influenced this book that I'd like to recognize. Throughout the book, I quote numerous people and cite news stories, and personal experiences to bring into the story as many perspectives as possible. I also draw on the expertise of hundreds of smart, interesting people in public relations, social media, advertising, branding, corporate communications, and marketing through my Twitter, Facebook, and LinkedIn networks. Any time, day or night, I could ask a question like "what trends will define the next generation of social media?" and know I would get a dozen useful, informed responses that all ended up influencing the book.

One of the definitions of "social" is "a tendency to move or live together in a group." "Social" in social media refers to the ability of this technology to bring people together and to change they way they interact. No examination of the field of social media would be complete without recognizing the people who made it possible and in fact, would be a sham. Thank you, then, to all of the people who helped make this book what it is.

Contents

Socializing Corporate Communications

The world of communications is changing dramatically with the introduction of the social media phenomenon. CEOs are having one-on-one conversations with customers. Consumers are providing direct input into the design of the products and services they use. Conventional definitions of news, journalism, and commentary no longer apply.

You may be asking, "What does all of this mean for the corporate communications professional? How is it relevant to me? What are the benefits of introducing social media in my company? How do I design and measure successful social media initiatives? Are there any risks or barriers to success associated with using social media in corporate communications, and how do I mitigate these?"

This book will answer these questions, explain the fundamentals of social media, and more importantly, how and *why* you should be using it to improve corporate communications.

If your job involves developing and implementing social media programs, this book will help. Even if you don't have daily responsibility for social media today, as a business professional, you should understand it, as it will only continue to grow in importance in the corporate world. If you're a rising executive, and you want to hone your business skills to make yourself more productive and more valuable to your organization, social media literacy is critical to success. A basic understanding of social media, and the ability to use a few social networks and other tools correctly, is the new basic business skills, alongside PowerPoint and presentation skills and the ability to create and understand an Excel spreadsheet.

Social media is everywhere. Social networks MySpace and Facebook each claim over 100 million users as of mid-2008. At the same time, blog search site Technorati was tracking 133 million blogs. And according to a comScore research report, two out of every three Internet users regularly visit a social networking site, and "the number of worldwide visitors to social networking sites has grown 34 percent in the past year to 530 million." In some regions, such as the UK, social networking sites account for more than 75 percent of all web traffic.

These numbers, and what they imply, are undeniable. There is no question that social media has arrived as a mainstream communications tool.

Yet social media is still new or foreign to many. I was speaking at a conference of PR professionals, and one of the participants asked, "what is a blog?" A few people chuckled. But I saw this as a wonderful opportunity. Social media has been around for a while. But to be fair, even those who are comfortable with it and use it on a daily basis might be hard-pressed to tell you what it is, how best to use it, or even why you would want to use it at all. The question "what is a blog?" is one of many starting points for this discussion. Without understanding each of the pieces that make up this thing we call social media, and how those pieces interact, it is impossible to understand its value or how you would use it in a corporate environment.

Social media is just another set of tools in the corporate communications toolbox. One of the things that makes these particular tools so powerful is the way they interact. So many of the social networks, websites, and tools available to the communicator have the capability to connect with each other in a way that exponentially increases their usefulness and impact. Combining several of these functions to create a more useful and compelling user experience is sometimes called a *mashup*. You can think of your corporate social media initiatives as mashups, as you combine capabilities and information from many sources. The beauty of the mashup is that for the first time, instead of being confined to the features that a single software vendor has decided are best for you (and everyone else in the world), you can pick and choose the capabilities you need from dozens of sources, to create social media tools best suited to your requirements.

Social media is rich in buzzwords, acronyms, and technical and pseudo-technical terms. You may at first be overwhelmed by the swirl of new and arcane terminology you encounter. Throughout the book, a great many of these terms are either defined directly or in the Glossary. The Glossary includes terms used in the book and others not mentioned to help you navigate through your adventures in social media. A quick note on singular/plural nouns. The previous paragraph begins, "Social media is..." It's unclear whether social media required the singular or plural verb form. (People still argue over "data is" vs. "data are"). Both forms are used in this book. When social media is referring to a set of tools, it is treated as a plural noun. When it is being applied as a concept, however, it is treated as a singular noun. Most of the time.

And while you don't need to be technically inclined to be a social media leader, you do need to be able to properly use a few technical terms in order to get the respect and cooperation of the people in your IT organization who can make or break your social media implementations. Once, as I worked on the launch of an executive podcasting (audio blog) program, IT kept telling me the company's blog wouldn't support podcasting. I asked enough people why this was and eventually learned it was because the blogging software "didn't support RSS 2.0 enclosures." That was all I needed to know. I did some research and found some people in the IT organization who knew something about RSS 2.0 enclosures. They found a workaround, and we were off and running. Did it matter I had no idea what RSS 2.0 enclosures were? Not at all. I call this "knowing enough to be dangerous," which is what you'll know about the technical aspects of social media after you read this book.

The book is laid out, as closely as possible, in the order a typical communicator might follow in developing a social media program. You'll gain first a general understanding of social media, followed by more specifics regarding social media tools and applications, and finally, you'll learn how real companies are using these tools for serious business communications.

In the first two chapters, "Social Media Goes Corporate" and "What Does It Take to Become a SocialCorp?," you'll learn about what it is to be a Social-Corp and why your company should be one. The SocialCorp Readiness Quiz will help you assess your company's culture, capabilities, leadership, and organizational structure, and how they might influence the adoption and success of social media.

After that, in Chapter 3, "What Are Social Media and Web 2.0?," you'll tackle the twin phenomenon of social media and Web 2.0, two terms to which each could have an entire book devoted, and learn how they interact in a way that has forever changed the world of communications. Chapter 3 not only defines popular social media terms, but explains the concepts behind them and how they interconnect and influence each other. You'll gain more than enough understanding of social media fundamentals to be able to hold your own in any corporate discussion.

You may also have heard that you no longer "own" your company's brand (or that you never did), and control has been ceded to the marketplace. Chapter 4, "Can You Control Your Brand or Just Share It?," offers a contemporary definition of the "brand," and suggestions for letting go of the brand in some cases, and gently managing it in others.

Chapter 5, "Using Social Media to Reach the Right People," features case studies and examples of how companies are using social media "beyond the blog" to reach employees, shareholders, business partners, and other important people.

Social media adoption in a corporate environment is not without its challenges and risks. Many of the things that make social media so compelling, like authenticity, transparency, and openness, may be difficult to reproduce in the corporate communications lab. Can you imagine the CEO of a publicly held company being 100 percent open, transparent, and honest about the company's finances? Today's CEO operates in a highly visible, highly regulated environment. Failure to properly report the company's finances in accordance with accounting standards, or conversely, talking about the company's finances during quiet periods and other times when to do so is prohibited, could land a CEO in jail.

In addition, when you're operating under the watchful eyes of external regulators like the SEC, FTC, and EU, corporate communications initiatives must often involve the oversight of internal functions like legal, finance, and branding. Chapter 6, "Balancing Social Media Risk and Reward," reviews the current legal and ethical climate and offers advice on how to implement successful, effective social media initiatives while remaining mindful of the company's broader obligations.

There are case studies and examples throughout the book. Some of these were created specifically for the book, and others came from existing sources online and elsewhere. These are useful in making real the many ways in which social media can be adopted in a large corporation. Not all of them, of course, will work in your company. Your choice of which tool you use, and how, will be dictated by your communications and business objectives.

Throughout the book are references to the need to tie social media strategy to communication strategy, which supports business strategy and objectives. That may seem a little old-fashioned and heavy-handed, but in a demanding economic environment like the one we're in, companies don't have the luxury of embarking on new initiatives that are not going to help the company get where it needs to go.

Which brings us to Chapter 7, "Can You Count Everything That Counts?" This chapter draws its name from something Albert Einstein once said, "Not everything that can be counted counts, and not everything that counts can be counted." This is probably as good a way as any to describe the difficulty in accurately assessing the success of corporate social media. Every program rolled out in a corporate environment is subject to measurement and requires constant improvement. Social media is no exception. However, this is an emerging field, and it's still very difficult to tie "hard" business metrics like revenue and margin directly to social media initiatives. There are, however, as you will see in Chapter 7, many, many approaches to measuring social media effectiveness.

And finally Chapter 8, "SocialCorp 2.0: Corporate Communications Inside Out," looks at a few of the more "bleeding edge" trends in social media that will be interesting to watch in the next 12 to 18 months, and which will influence the kinds of social media programs you'll be planning for the future.

Users, for example, are demonstrating shorter and shorter attention spans. Fewer and fewer are willing to read full-length articles online or off. Video is most popular in short "clip" format, generally three minutes or less in length. This new trend toward brevity has implications for the next round of popular social media tools.

Virtual reality worlds like Second Life and Google's Lively have potential as corporate communications tools, yet they have not yet achieved mainstream adoption.

If you read this book, you'll be ahead of 95 percent of your "competitors," including both competitive companies and those competing with you for promotions and career advancement, but only for a short while. Things are moving so quickly that once you finish the book and understand its concepts, your very next step will be to grow your understanding of social media trends and the tools and specific corporate applications that are the most effective in the corporate world.

There will be other books, and you should attend relevant conferences and take classes, both "live" and via the web. And there are hundreds of online resources.

As you gain better command of your social networking skills, you'll meet dozens, possibly hundreds, of colleagues around the world grappling with the same opportunities and challenges you are facing. As you improve your company's social media programs, you'll develop a network of like-minded professionals, many of whom you may actually meet along the way, or who might even become lifelong friends. If you learn anything from the book, please pass it on to your network. And look for me. I'm out there, and I would be grateful to hear your thoughts on what it takes to become a Social-Corp and how you did it.

Joel Postman

Social Media Goes Corporate

Tony Hsieh, CEO of Zappos, "hangs out" on microblogging site Twitter and chats one-on-one with consumers about everything from their favorite styles of shoes to ideas about the company's philanthropic goals. The CEO of BlendTec, a company that makes high-end blenders (yes, the kind you'd use to make a smoothie or a margarita) produces inexpensive videos in which he demonstrates the power of his company's products by blending iPhones, ballpoint pens, lightsticks, and other objects. Silly? Maybe, but the company's videos draw millions of viewers, translating into brand awareness, traffic to BlendTec's website, and revenue.

Computer giant Dell has received close to 10,000 ideas from customers through its IdeaStorm website. The company publishes those ideas and reports on which ideas it intends to implement and its progress toward doing so. Dell estimates that through its various communications channels the company has two billion "conversations" with customers every year.

Can you imagine even a few years ago, a CEO spending a Sunday chatting directly with consumers about company strategy? Or a company marketing its products by putting household objects into a blender? Or an IT company opening a website to any and all comers, not only asking for their ideas, but putting them into practice?

Social media, once thought of as the domain of kids with crazy MySpace pages and college students publicly announcing they are looking for "whatever I can get" on Facebook, has made its way into the communications strategies of the world's largest companies.

We're still in the early days of corporate adoption of social media, but clearly it's time for business people to join in the revolution and reap the benefits.

Of course, it's more complex to accomplish this in a large corporation, and that's where this book comes in. While the conversational aspects and audience engagement value of social media are well understood, many theorists often overlook the realities faced by the large corporation, like accountability to shareholders and regulators. These factors cannot be overlooked in corporate social media adoption.

This book will help companies of all sizes develop and implement a strategy to become a *SocialCorp*, a progressive, forward-thinking company that has adopted social media effectively, in a way that accomplishes strategic business and communications objectives without compromising the company's primary obligations as a corporation.

Using case studies, a survey of available social media tools, and proven corporate social media strategies, the book will help corporate communicators understand the new communications landscape, the power of social media, and how to adopt it in a corporate environment.

To highlight both the benefits and challenges of these communications tools, SocialCorp will draw on the work of in-house and agency communications professionals who have done outstanding work in corporate social media.

It is quite simply a revolution in communications that businesses of all sizes cannot afford to ignore. It's time for your company to become a SocialCorp.

What Is a SocialCorp?

Dell, Zappos, IBM, Proctor and Gamble, and dozens of other industry leaders are SocialCorps, companies that are learning to take advantage of the power of social media to reshape their relationships with customers and other important audiences. (Some social media purists balk at the "antiquated" notion of audiences. This book does not. More on that later.) They have the culture, the organizational structure, the creativity, and the talent to exploit new communications tools for unparalleled transparency, authenticity, and immediacy. They are reaching customers, journalists, bloggers, analysts, shareholders, employees, and business partners more often, in larger numbers, more intimately, and more effectively than ever before.

Why Your Company Should Become a SocialCorp

There are many benefits, some easier to quantify than others, to being a SocialCorp. Let's take a look at eight of these benefits.

Unparalleled Access to Information

A SocialCorp is tapped into an incredible body of information—consumer buying habits, brand perception, the competitive landscape, and product support issues—that is invaluable in making informed decisions by which to run the company.

Enhanced Brand Awareness and Perception

Social media are a set of tools to add to the corporate communications mix. In addition to helping companies distribute their messages across hundreds or even thousands of outlets, social media enables genuine 1:1 conversations with consumers.

A company can improve its brand perception by being better engaged with so-called "influencers," like customers, employees, bloggers, and journalists, and being seen as connected to, and interested in, what's going on outside the company's four walls. Consumers also recognize that social media is a new direction for corporate communications and see companies that use social media as creative, willing to take risks, and forward thinking.

Better Engagement with Customers, Employees, and Business Partners

A SocialCorp is able to engage with influencers in a more intimate and audience-specific way. By creating social media initiatives specifically for each audience and engaging them on their terms in a way that is relevant to them, the company improves its communications effectiveness. The participatory nature of social media lets everyone associated with the company play a more active role in shaping the company's strategy. Customers who engage with the company through *well-designed and implemented* social media feel they are being listened to and that the company cares about them and their satisfaction.

Collaboration

Certain kinds of social media, like wikis and online communities, enable new levels of collaboration. The relationships developed through these kinds of tools can live both inside and outside of company walls. Some companies' product management and engineering teams are using wikis internally to improve communications and streamline product development. Other companies are using forums to enlist customer opinion on upcoming products and solicit suggestions for improvements to current product lines, and they're using collaboration tools to improve communications and workflow with external developers and business partners.

Richer User Experience

At a tactical level, a SocialCorp can provide visitors to its blogs, websites and communities, external and internal, with an improved user experience through rich media and other technologies. Social media, with its Web 2.0 foundation, enables the use of streaming and archival video, easily browsed image libraries, podcasts, and more. Linking is simpler, making it easier to offer access to external resources. Tagging helps organize information by topic and audience to make it easier to find things. Social bookmarking allows visitors to share information from the company's site with other online users.

Industry surveys show again and again that users prefer a rich media experience to visiting a text-heavy site, and that video in particular draws them to a site, keeps them there longer, and influences purchasing decisions. Many companies find that social media and Web 2.0 technology enable them to deliver user experiences their conventional websites and intranet sites cannot.

Improved Web Metrics

The well-run company uses both *hard* measures, like revenue and lead generation, and *soft* measures, like brand perception and engagement, to gauge the effectiveness of its communications efforts, and social media is no exception. While the market for enterprise-grade tools for measuring social media effectiveness is in its early stages, a number of companies, including Radian6 and BuzzLogic, are offering tools for measuring social media site traffic and visitor behavior, as well as providing certain measures of external effectiveness. Good social media programs can deliver measurable improvements in site traffic and even conversion (click-through to a sale.)

Increased Control over the Company's Marketplace Message

An interesting paradox exists in a SocialCorp. In an era in which we are being told that consumers control the company's brand, and we have to "let go" of the company's message, the SocialCorp, with its command of social media tools and understanding of the environment, can actually *better* control its message by participating intelligently in social media instead of ignoring it. Whether you choose to participate or not, there's a conversation going on out there about your company, and the only way to maintain any control over your message is to participate in the conversation.

Perhaps the most overused and underexplained word in social media is *conversation*. But this concept is an important part of understanding the philosophy and therefore taking advantage of social media's power.

"The Conversation"

A significant aspect of social media is its ability to take advantage of the dramatic changes in the way people use the Internet—changes in the way they communicate, meet new friends, learn about and purchase products, enjoy entertainment, and in the very fundamental ways they live their lives.

The Cluetrain Manifesto (Perseus Publishing, 2000), written by Rick Levine, Christopher Locke, Doc Searls, and David Weinberger, is perhaps the bible of the philosophy of social media in general, and is one of the earliest books to identify the concept of the global online conversation.

> "On the Internet, markets are getting more connected and more powerfully vocal every day. These markets want to talk, just as they did for the thousands of years that passed before market became a verb with us as its object.

The Internet is a place. We buy books and tickets on the Web. Not over, through, or beside it. ...The Net is a real place where people can go to learn, to talk to each other, and to do business together. It is a bazaar where customers look for wares, vendors spread goods for display, and people gather around topics that interest them. It is a conversation."

This concept is prophetic in its predictions and stunning in its clarity. True, we had Web 1.0 or whatever you want to call it in 2000 when the book was published, but neither the terms *social media* or *Web 2.0*, or any of the advances associated with them, had been introduced for mainstream use. The authors clearly foresaw the incredible way that MySpace, Facebook, You-Tube, and so on would transform the world of communications.

This new generation of technology, content, websites, and online applications called social media has changed communications forever, giving companies and consumers the power to actually converse with each other like never before. Social media, done properly, is the closest thing yet to one-on-one conversation between even the largest companies and the millions of people they do business with.

It is also a conversation in which anyone can participate. While celebrity still plays a role, particularly in terms of which blogs are considered the most influential, anyone with something interesting and relevant to contribute can get into the conversation. It is, as blogging superstar and former Microsoft uber blogger Robert Scoble said, a world in which "some fifteen-year-old kid in Australia" has just as much opportunity to be at the top of the day's news as does CNN.

And while many people associate corporate social media with executive blogs, there are dozens of other social media tools and strategies companies can adopt, including video and podcasting, online communities, wikis, microblogging, and social networking, to participate in that conversation.

We'll take a more detailed look in Chapter 3, "What Are Social Media and Web 2.0?," at the vast number of social media and Web 2.0 tools companies are using, but first, let's briefly look at why—and how—social media and Web 2.0 can help your company become a SocialCorp.

Social Media and Web 2.0

In the past five years or so, the Internet got an upgrade, and it's completely changed the way people are working, communicating, and living. This new

Internet is fueled by a new class of online content, applications, and services called social media, and made possible by underlying technology infrastructure called *Web 2.0*.

To understand this phenomenon, it's worth understanding the terms *Web 2.0* and *social media*. *Social media* are the latest generation of network-based applications and content that have brought about a revolution in participatory communications, building communities and creating and sharing information. Social networks like Facebook and MySpace; blogs; photo sharing sites like Flickr and Photobucket; online communities; microblogging tools like Twitter; social bookmarking services like Digg; newsreaders like Net-Vibes and Google Reader; and video creation and sharing services like Qik, Seesmic, YouTube, and Ustream.TV are all examples of social media. With these services, users can post, share, and comment on text, images, audio, and video, generally in moments, and with no technical knowledge. What's really amazing is that these services not only allow sharing content on the web, but they can actually share with each other, despite, in most cases, being independently owned and managed.

All of this is made possible by Web 2.0 technology, the latest generation of web infrastructure. The phrase was most likely coined by Tim O'Reilly, when he organized the first Web 2.0 Conference in October, 2004, to encourage technologists to speculate about the next generation of the web. Web 2.0 has come to refer to a set of technological innovations that make it possible for applications to share information, for people to subscribe to news alerts and feeds, for adding video to web pages, and so on.

The geeks will tell you that the key to Web 2.0 is AJAX (Asynchronous JavaScript and XML). All you need to know is that together, these technologies make all kinds of things possible.

This Is Not Your Father's Corporate Communications

Earlier, I mentioned some of the underlying notions of social media—that all the rules have changed, that complete transparency and authenticity are the hallmarks of effective communications, that companies no longer "own" their brands, and that consumers have taken over.

But how do you incorporate these values in a communications strategy that still makes sense in the corporate world? Yes, the goals of corporate social media are much the same as those of social media in general, but complete "brand surrender" doesn't make sense.

In some sense, your brand is your company. And the notion that you have to surrender your brand isn't consistent with growing your business and differentiating your company and its products and services in a competitive marketplace. In truth, your customers have always "owned" your brand. Your brand is the sum total of their experiences with your company and its products, your customer service, and the ways (good and bad) your company changes their lives. This is nothing new. The difference with social media is that you can listen to millions of people and learn, day-by-day, how your brand is performing, where your company is strong, and where you have work to do; and then, you can join in the conversation and positively influence your brand for the better.

A.G. Lafley, the CEO of consumer products giant Proctor and Gamble, gave a keynote address at an advertising industry conference, in which he said, "consumers are beginning in a very real sense to own our brands and participate in their creation. We need to learn to begin to let go." This is an interesting and game-changing observation from the CEO of a company that essentially created the position of "brand manager."

On the path to becoming a SocialCorp, your company will need to, as Lafley says, "begin to let go" of your brand. But don't worry, you won't have to surrender it. An integrated companywide social media strategy will help you decide just how much "control" you want to let go of and how you can manage your company's social media initiatives to achieve business results like improved brand perception and awareness.

Six Valuable Attributes of Social Media

There are six key attributes of social media that make it a powerful tool in corporate communications:

- Authenticity

- Transparency

- Immediacy

- Participation

- Connectedness

- Accountability

Let's look at how social media embodies these attributes and why that matters to you.

AUTHENTICITY

Perhaps the most powerful attribute of social media is authenticity. Never before in the history of corporate communications have we seen so much unfiltered, unmassaged, spontaneous information coming directly from the people that run the world's largest corporations.

As one of social media's holy grails, authenticity is something that needs to be actively championed in the corporation. I don't want this to sound like a story line from *The X Files*, but there are dark forces that are conspiring within your organization to reduce the authenticity of your social media initiatives. OK, maybe its not that sinister, but legal, with its mission to protect the corporation and mitigate risk; marketing, with its goal of maintaining messaging purity; and sales, which is traditionally measured on revenue and margin, may all have agendas that conflict with authenticity and other core values of social media. This book will help you understand the importance of being authentic and the risk to your company's reputation if you are not. The book will also show you how to work with every function in the company to develop a winning social media strategy.

TRANSPARENCY

Transparency really has two closely related meanings in a corporate social media environment. The first is transparency in the *traditional* sense, as used in finance. The use of transparency in this sense became widespread in the aftermath of the scandals and business failures of the dot-com crash. These events launched corporate financial *transparency* into the forefront of our culture's consciousness. Transparency calls for the removal of all barriers to free, timely public access to accurate information on a company's finances, ownership, and business prospects. Probably the most important regulations governing corporate transparency include the Securities and Exchange Commission's (SEC) Regulation Fair Disclosure (Reg FD), Sarbanes-Oxley, and the Financial Accounting Standards Board (FASB), which govern the format, standards, and timing for the disclosure of financial information in a publicly held company.

Social media can be a valuable tool for complying with these regulations. In August, 2008, the SEC announced that it was time to bring financial reporting into the twenty-first century, and the commission would agree to accept some forms of website postings in lieu of more traditional quarterly communications required of publicly held companies. Given the complexity of the rules, and the SEC's traditional stance on these kinds of communications, this is truly a watershed event in corporate social media.

In addition to financial transparency, social media can also provide complete transparency into a company's strategy, its progress toward meeting its goals, and its "thinking" about its products, services, markets, customers, and even broader issues like the environment and corporate social responsibility. As we'll see later, companies are taking a chance and exposing every aspect of their business to public scrutiny to create closer and more fruitful relationships with customers, employees, business partners, and others.

IMMEDIACY

Social media lets communications happen at lightning fast speed. The tools available today to update a blog, community, or website, or to create and upload video, allow nontechnical communications people and others to create content and publish it on the web in a matter of minutes or moments. This has important implications in corporate communications, particularly in crisis communications and other "breaking news" situations.

On the positive side, communications is now more current and more relevant. In the past, the production process was a barrier to rapid communications, and combined with the typical corporate content review process, made immediate news publication almost impossible. If you wanted to post something to the company's website, you first had to draft the message and circulate it for reviews by both the communications team (at multiple levels) as well as legal and in some cases finance and/or investor relations. This hasn't changed. What has changed is what happens next. Instead of sending the message to the web team for HTML coding, anyone with access to the company's blog or social media *newsroom* (a social media–enabled update on the traditional corporate website news page) can instantly post the message simply by copying and pasting it from a document into an editing screen and clicking publish. Since most editing and authoring tools are web-based, you don't need to be inside the corporate firewall to publish. Adding images, videos, and links also takes just a few seconds. It's true that many companies have sophisticated content management systems (CMS) with many of these capabilities, but they are not general-use authoring tools.

This immediacy also happens in areas beyond the company's control, particularly in external blogs, communities, and social networks where anyone can make a negative (or positive) comment or report on news affecting the company. For this reason, corporate communicators should use the tools mentioned in Chapter 3 to monitor the blogosphere conversation, because there's always the chance that breaking news relevant to the company will be published outside of "normal" communications channels and without the knowledge of the corporation.

Social media, and the community that uses it, are so fast that news often breaks online first. In July, 2008, for example, a 5.4 magnitude earthquake hit Southern California near Los Angeles. Initial reports of the quake were on Twitter, well ahead of the traditional media.

PARTICIPATION

The degree to which external audiences now participate in corporate communications is truly revolutionary. This participation comes in many forms. On a company's blog or social media newsroom, visitors can leave comments and ask questions about specific blog posts and news items. In the customer forums, consumers can post discussion topics and ask questions, with other consumers often joining the discussion and providing the answers. Many consumer forums are nearly self running, in that people who are experienced with the company's products often become experts and evangelists for the products and in many cases are more than happy to spend their time on providing a new kind of customer support, by and for customers. Consumers are very enthusiastic about the opportunity to be heard by the companies they do business with and to share their experiences with others.

Like nearly every aspect of social media, this new level of participation brings with it both benefits and risks. The most obvious risk with participation is that, in a simplified way, consumers can use commenting and forums to post directly to your public website. There are ways to mitigate this risk, such as comment moderation and content submission policies, which will be covered later in the book.

In general, however, the benefits of two-way conversation far outweigh the minimal risks of this new heightened level of participation. As previously mentioned, companies like Dell are encouraging consumers to contribute ideas for new products and services and having other consumers weigh in on these ideas. This not only lets consumers feel like they have a real voice in how the company designs its products, but it enhances the company's brand in general. Companies that have the willingness and creativity to explore these new avenues for conversation are seen as humble, open-minded, and genuinely engaged with their customers.

CONNECTEDNESS

Another aspect of social media, closely related to immediacy, is connectedness. Not only does communications happen faster, but with the Web 2.0 infrastructure, it is also more widely distributed.

With RSS feeds that instantly send company news to thousands of readers the instant it is published, alerts that let people know when something has been posted to a company site, and thousands of bloggers linking to, bookmarking, and commenting on company news, the moment something is published to a company social media site, it's gone out to thousands of people.

In the past, you added keywords and meta tags to a web page, maybe bought keywords from a search engine (you all know who I am talking about, I can only put the "G" word in the book so many times), posted your content, and waited for the search engines' automated web "spiders" to find it. If your social media applications are configured correctly, it can be just moments before people are aware of new content. Again, this is a good thing and a bad thing.

I once witnessed this first-hand supporting a client during a crisis communications situation. The agency I was at managed the company's blog and received a CEO blog post from corporate communications with a request that we publish the post immediately (or at least that's what we thought the request said). We did so, and within about two minutes, I heard back from my boss asking why we published the post. Apparently, the post had not been approved by all the necessary reviewers. (I know, it's shocking, but in some situations blog posts are actually reviewed.) In this case, the post was about a complicated stock situation, and there was no way we would put the client at legal risk by having the CEO simply attempt to explain the situation in his own words on his blog without a review by investor relations.

My boss knew the post had been published because she had set up a Google alert to let her know the moment anything was posted anywhere with the company's name in it, so she got an email on her Blackberry just moments after we clicked the publish button. This proved both the efficiency of Web 2.0 infrastructure to get a message out to multiple points almost instantaneously and the need to have appropriate review processes and controls in place.

ACCOUNTABILITY

Often on the web, you see examples of antisocial, and sometimes unethical or illegal, behavior exhibited by users participating in online forums and chat rooms, and by leaving comments on blogs, videos, and so on. This phenomenon is very common on YouTube, where comments can be highly negative, and sometimes downright vicious. There are many reasons for this. Many people believe they are anonymous online, and they ignore the regular social graces they would practice in "real life." Another is that bloggers and people who leave comments who employ controversy and negativity are often rewarded in the form of site traffic and "recognition."

Misrepresentation is also common online. Years ago a number of jokes went around about this. One said that no one knows you're a dog on the Internet, and another said that the cheerleader you met in a chat room is probably a trucker in his 40s. Not that there's anything wrong with truckers in their 40s, but communications is a lot easier when you know who you're talking with.

Most of the notions underlying the idea that you can hide your identity online are false. There have been many cases in which corporations have used social media in less than aboveboard ways, hoping to impress consumers or gain a competitive edge. In one high-profile case, John Mackey, the CEO of Whole Foods, participated anonymously in Yahoo finance forums, denigrating a competitor, Wild Oats markets, at the same time Whole Foods was in negotiations to acquire Wild Oats. In this case, heated speculation around the identity of the mysterious Rahodeb (Mackey's online name, and an anagram of his wife's name) resulted in Mackey's confession.

In many cases, social media falsehoods are rooted out by consumers or those in the social media field. In August 2008, Twitter users were excited to learn that ExxonMobil had a company representative answering consumer questions on the service. Blogger and Forrester analyst Jeremiah Owyang placed a call to ExxonMobil and found that its so-called representative on Twitter was unknown to them and not an authorized representative of the company. In other cases, the perpetrators of online deception have been very easy to find using technology (found in most blogging and other social media software) that captures every user's unique IP address, which can help identify the companies they work for and where the online communications originated from.

While technological solutions and community oversight do provide social media with a fairly high degree of accountability, these will not be enough in the long run to give consumers the level of trust required if these tools are to be used successfully by corporations. This new, enhanced level of trust will come from several places. Online media associations have made numerous attempts at issuing social media ethics guidelines, but sadly, without enforcement, violations of even the simplest guidelines will continue. Like any other emerging area of communications, regulators will step in. Already, the European Union has enacted legislation banning certain deceptive social media practices. Similar legislation is under consideration in the U.S. as well.

As in so many other areas of ethical concern, companies that use social media must instill ethical behavior in employees through training and policies and procedures, and above all, by maintaining an ethical culture.

Ultimately, ethical companies will behave ethically online, and consumers will reward those that do.

Social Media: Strategy or Tactic?

When asked about social media strategy, I often respond, "What's your Microsoft Word strategy? What's your email strategy?" The point is, all these things, social media included, are tools. You can type anything you want into a Microsoft Word document, and you can communicate anything you want to any audience through social media. They don't have inherent strategies, or at least, they do not have strategies that stand on their own.

A key to success in corporate social media is to tie communications initiatives to business strategy. Increasingly, we are seeing large corporations creating social media (sometimes under the banner of "new media" or "digital media") leadership positions to oversee companywide strategy and implementation across all functions. To mention a few, Ford Motor Company has Scott Monty as its Digital and Multimedia Communications Manager; Jeanette Gibson is Director of New Media for Cisco Systems; and at Nationwide Insurance, Shawn Morton is Senior Consultant for Social Media.

What every one of them will most likely tell you is that social media needs to be part of a broader business strategy, requiring the participation of numerous functions inside the company. The company may either decide on a centralized approach, with the identification of social media leaders, or it may take a distributed approach, deciding that every function needs to become social media literate. The best strategy incorporates both approaches.

Often, you'll need to make the case for social media by demonstrating to each function within the company how it can benefit from its use and how you will mitigate perceived risk. Broad, early collaboration and sensitivity to the goals and concerns of every function in the company will greatly speed social media adoption and success.

Strategy Basics

To apply the right communications tactics to a business situation, you need a communications strategy. And a communications strategy needs to help the company achieve its business objectives.

Particularly in the early days of social media adoption, it's OK in some cases to embark on initiatives without clearly defined revenue goals or other traditional goals, which are often very hard to measure. And there is something to be said for being creative and for being willing to take a chance and experiment in a controlled environment, like a limited foray into Facebook or Second Life. But overall, your company will expect social media to have some connections to its business strategy.

There are many components of a successful social media strategy, which we will look at in greater depth later in the book, but here are some that should be included in every plan:

- **Social media platform:** Define key audiences, messages, channels, and appropriate company spokespeople.

- **Social network strategy:** Evaluate Twitter, Facebook, MySpace, and other social networks as company social media vehicles.

- **Cross-functional implementation:** Develop a framework and processes for ensuring that all appropriate company functions participate in the development, implementation, and ongoing management of social media initiatives.

- **Tools review:** Analyze and select social media tools, like blog and wiki platforms and video players, that meet the company's objectives and can be integrated with the company's IT environment.

- **Editorial strategy:** Implement "lightweight" oversight to ensure that owners of social media initiatives are aware of and are appropriately adopting marketing and other company messages.

- **Training:** Conduct training for all levels of the organization in social media strategy, philosophy, and etiquette, as well as hands-on use of the company's social media tools and networks.

- **Policies:** Develop agreements and codes of ethics for social media usage consistent with company policies to reduce risk and ensure ethical compliance.

- **Social media analysis:** Review social media use by competitors, influencers (like bloggers and analysts), and business partners.

- **Social media council:** Create an in-house team dedicated to regularly scheduled review, recommendations, and enforcement of policies for social media programs.

- **Measurement:** Define methods to evaluate and regularly measure success for each initiative.

While some companies look at the tools first and ask, "should we be on Facebook?," it's more productive to approach social media from a traditional communications standpoint and consider each tool and social network in the context of whether it's the right medium for the audience, the message, the budget, and the company's objectives.

Let's say your company makes specialized integrated circuits for the video gaming industry. Your business objective for the first half is to build a developer base for a new chip. You could launch an online community for video gamers, which would be really cool, and if successful, could drive thousands of people to your site. But what would that do to persuade developers to adopt your technology? Maybe you would be better off building a developer community first and reaching out to gamers later in the adoption cycle.

Social media strategy isn't that complex, but it does require a synthesis of traditional thinking, creativity, understanding of new tools and etiquette, and the willingness to take some chances. The tricky part is that too much strategy, in the form of too many "gatekeepers" and too many policies and procedures, can kill the effectiveness of social media in a large corporation. You'll need to balance the virtues of "pure" social media we talked about earlier with the desire of certain forces within the company to maintain control.

Now What?

In the next chapter, you'll take the SocialCorp Readiness Quiz to see how your company measures up as a SocialCorp and how you can start down the path to making social media an indispensible and (more) powerful part of your communications mix.

What Does It Take to Become a SocialCorp?

Your company's culture, leadership, communications strategy, industry, and other factors will affect the adoption and success of your social media initiatives. The SocialCorp Readiness Quiz is intended primarily to help you identify strengths and weaknesses in your company that should be factored in the formulation of your social media strategy, but is also useful for assessing companies with social media programs already in place.

SocialCorp Readiness Quiz

This quiz will help you rate your company's social media readiness in six key areas. As you take the quiz you'll detect certain themes. Feel free to make copies and share it with colleagues. The quiz is available as a free download at www.social-corp.com/quiz. After you finish the quiz, review your responses and see where your company is strong, where it needs to improve, and why. For each question, rate your response in any of the boxes, from left to right, with the far left box indicating the highest level of agreement, and the far right box indicating the highest level of disagreement with the statement.

Leadership

1. Is your company's leadership open to trying new communications strategies and tools?

   Yes 5 ☐   4 ☐   3 ☐   2 ☐   1 ☐   0 ☐ No

2. Does your leadership value the opinions of younger employees?

   Yes 5 ☐   4 ☐   3 ☐   2 ☐   1 ☐   0 ☐ No

3. Are there people in your company whose sole responsibility is social media strategy and policy?

   Yes 5 ☐   4 ☐   3 ☐   2 ☐   1 ☐   0 ☐ No

Innovation

4. Does your company reward entrepreneurial behavior within the organization?

   Yes 5 ☐   4 ☐   3 ☐   2 ☐   1 ☐   0 ☐ No

5. Is it possible for employees to research and implement new initiatives outside their formal job descriptions?

   Yes 5 ☐   4 ☐   3 ☐   2 ☐   1 ☐   0 ☐ No

6. Do you have a progressive IT organization that will work with you to deploy the software and infrastructure required for your social media initiatives?

   Yes 5 ☐   4 ☐   3 ☐   2 ☐   1 ☐   0 ☐ No

Industry

7. Have other companies in your industry successfully used social media in corporate communications or marketing?

   Yes   5 □   4 □   3 □   2 □   1 □   0 □   No

8. Are you in a highly regulated industry, such as financial services or pharmaceuticals, in which extra caution is required in your communications programs?

   Yes   0 □   1 □   2 □   3 □   4 □   5 □   No

Business Objectives

9. Would your company benefit from more cross-functional team collaboration?

   Yes   5 □   4 □   3 □   2 □   1 □   0 □   No

10. Do you use the results of focus groups, surveys, and other customer data to make changes to your products, processes, and policies?

    Yes   5 □   4 □   3 □   2 □   1 □   0 □   No

11. Does your management evaluate the success of your communications initiatives solely on traditional business metrics, like revenue and margin?

    Yes   0 □   1 □   2 □   3 □   4 □   5 □   No

Engagement

12. Do you actively monitor what's being "said" about the company through traditional channels, such as print media?

    Yes   5 □   4 □   3 □   2 □   1 □   0 □   No

13. Do you actively monitor what's being "said" about the company through Web 2.0/social media channels, such as blogs, social networks, and online communities?

    Yes   5 □   4 □   3 □   2 □   1 □   0 □   No

14. Do you respond to negative "buzz" about the company?

    Yes   5 □   4 □   3 □   2 □   1 □   0 □   No

15. Do your customers consider peer reviews or word of mouth in purchasing products like yours?

    Yes   5 ☐   4 ☐   3 ☐   2 ☐   1 ☐   0 ☐   **No**

Culture

16. Do your clients and customers currently use social media for business purposes?

    Yes   5 ☐   4 ☐   3 ☐   2 ☐   1 ☐   0 ☐   **No**

17. Are your employees active on Facebook, MySpace, or other social networks?

    Yes   5 ☐   4 ☐   3 ☐   2 ☐   1 ☐   0 ☐   **No**

18. Does anyone within the company blog on business-related issues?

    Yes   5 ☐   4 ☐   3 ☐   2 ☐   1 ☐   0 ☐   **No**

19. Do any of your company's social media "experts" participate in external conferences on subjects like social media, corporate communications, or Web 2.0?

    Yes   5 ☐   4 ☐   3 ☐   2 ☐   1 ☐   0 ☐   **No**

20. Does your company embrace less formal communication with the outside world without the involvement of legal, marketing, and PR departments?

    Yes   5 ☐   4 ☐   3 ☐   2 ☐   1 ☐   0 ☐   **No**

Score

This quiz is intended only to give you an overview of the kinds of things that will affect your company's ability to adopt and take advantage of social media. Once you've identified any areas of concern, formal research—like surveys, focus groups, market research, analyst input, and competitive analysis—will help you more accurately define the steps you need to take to become a true SocialCorp.

Use the following scoring guidelines to help you determine your organization's readiness:

90–100: Your company is already a SocialCorp. Congratulations. Please submit a case study for inclusion in the next edition of this book.

80–89: You have the right culture, leadership, and other conditions in place to allow your company to become a SocialCorp, with great potential for broad social media adoption.

70–79: The fundamentals are good, and you're well on your way to becoming a SocialCorp, but to be successful you'll need to carefully factor those areas in which the company might not be perfectly aligned for success.

Below 70: Don't despair. Your responses indicate only that there are some barriers to social media adoption in your organization and that there might be certain social media strategies that won't work in your company or industry.

Next, let's look at what your responses to these questions tell you about your company's potential to be a SocialCorp.

SocialCorp Readiness

Now that you've taken the quiz, you've identified some characteristics of your company that will influence your social media strategy. The SocialCorp Readiness Quiz helped identify your company's strengths or weaknesses. This section expands on these factors and what you can do to influence them.

Leadership

1. Is your company's leadership open to trying new communications strategies and tools?

   Key to social media adoption is open-mindedness and willingness within the company's senior leadership. Think back, in a broad way, on the behavior of your senior management team over the past year. Have they demonstrated creativity and a willingness to take calculated risks in the initiatives they have adopted? Has the company expanded into new areas of business? At a macro level, what does the current communications "mix" look like, and how willing is your direct management to try new initiatives?

   As with any new strategy, you may have to "sell" social media to your organization. Once you have an idea of how you think your company can best employ social media, you should develop a social media strategy presentation and be prepared to "take it on the road" and give it numerous times to senior management and others in the organization who will influence your success.

2. Does your leadership value the opinions of younger employees?

There is an incredible wealth of social media experience within the company's four walls that will help you build a groundswell of support for the company's social media programs. At the risk of being ageist, to a large degree social media is a cult of youth, and the younger people in your organization will provide much of this expertise. They are so-called "digital natives" who grew up online, and most of them have used social networks extensively before joining the company. They also tend to have less inhibition when it comes to trying new online tools.

There are numerous ways to incorporate their insights into the company's social media strategy. You could, for example, conduct a social media readiness survey within the company, to assess what applications they believe would be useful inside and outside the company, and gauge their experience and comfort level. A statistically valid third-party survey might provide data of sufficient quality to motivate a stubborn senior management team to venture out into the world of social media.

If social media use is not yet pervasive in your company, there may be people who have embarked on small, ad hoc social media initiatives in the company, and their experience will be quite useful. These early initiatives could be made more visible to the senior executive team by including them in your social media strategy presentation. When appropriate, innovative use of social media inside the company might also be suitable for a mention on the company's intranet home page. Strategically, you will need the cooperation and buy-in of the social media pioneers within your company. You could invite them to be formal or informal members of your team and might consider bringing them along when you make your pitch to management.

3. Are there people in your company whose sole responsibility is social media strategy and policy?

More and more, companies are establishing an individual or an entire group with specific management responsibility for social media strategy and policy across the company. This does not relieve the other functions within the company, like marketing communications, public relations, and employee communications, from developing their own social media expertise, nor should it. Each organization will have specific objectives for their social media programs and will be best equipped to implement and manage them.

The function of a centralized role is rather:

- To develop and manage companywide social media policy to ensure compliance with applicable regulations and laws and the company's own guidelines and standards.

- To ensure that each function is aware of what others are doing, to leverage expertise and tools, and perhaps most importantly, to share content across social media vehicles.

- To serve as a clearinghouse for company social media resources.

- To engage with social media experts from the outside world to demonstrate the company's expertise and commitment and to learn from these experts.

Innovation

4. Does your company reward entrepreneurial behavior within the organization?

5. Is it possible for employees to research and implement new initiatives outside their formal job descriptions?

The degree to which the company encourages innovation and entrepreneurial behavior will directly affect the adoption of social media programs. According to the *New York Times*, "Google engineers are encouraged to take 20 percent of their time to work on something company-related that interests them personally. This means that if you have a great idea, you always have time to run with it...It sounds obvious, but people work better when they're involved in something they're passionate about, and many (of Google's) cool technologies have their origins in 20 percent time, including Gmail, Google News, and even the Google shuttle buses."

You've probably heard this story before, and it's equally probable that you don't work at Google. It's not the intent of this book to offer guidance on designing employee motivation programs but only to point out the importance of such programs in the adoption of any new strategy, technology, or communications tool. It wouldn't be one of your first steps, but if there are no such programs in your company, you should consider recommending one to senior management. It would not only free people to contribute to your social media programs, but it would benefit the entire organization.

In a typical "performance management" framework, it would be highly unusual for an employee to devote any significant amount of time and effort to developing social media programs unless that was a current job responsibility. Specific mechanisms, formal and informal, must be in place so that employees can explore these new communications tools not only without penalty but with the potential for the employee to receive reward and recognition for doing so. This is one of the most difficult situations to foster within a company, because it requires a specific commitment to allowing employees to pursue work that does not at the moment seem "mission critical." To not allow this kind of work would ultimately condemn a company to failure anyway, but there are those companies that don't operate this way, and they will find social media adoption to be awkward and difficult.

6. Do you have a progressive IT organization that will work with you to deploy the software and infrastructure required for your social media initiatives?

A good working relationship with your IT organization is perhaps the single most important factor affecting your ability to implement innovative social media programs. Oftentimes, simply having a single friendly contact in the IT organization will be enough for you to establish a beachhead.

The larger your company, the more complex (and often fixed) its IT infrastructure. The IT organization will generally have a predominant platform, operating system (such as Windows or Linux), security environment, and network and identity protocols. These will all influence IT's perception of what kinds of projects are possible. Note that in some cases these conclusions are realities and in other cases are simply perceptions that can be influenced. The story in the book's introduction of the "impossible" podcast that ended up taking less than 36 hours to implement is but one example of how, armed with a little bit of information, you can motivate your IT organization to "do the impossible."

The IT organization, and the web team, which plays a similar role, are among the people you need to influence with your social media strategy presentation. Let them know the kind of things you're considering and what you expect of them. To do that, you'll need to research the basic technical requirements for any specific software you have chosen, but you also need to be open-minded and listen to alternatives your IT organization might feel are easier and/or more beneficial to implement.

If you need additional help motivating your IT organization you can often do so with an executive sponsor. An executive sponsor is someone in the organization who carries some clout. Let's face it, as persuasive as you may be, and as important as your social media programs are, some people will be quicker to respond to you if they see it as an opportunity to make a good impression on a senior executive.

Industry

7. Have other companies in your industry successfully used social media in corporate communications or marketing?

   The examples and case studies in this book will show you how similar companies are using social media in corporate communications and marketing. Once you are familiar with the general state of corporate social media, you'll have a better idea of what might work in your company, and you'll be able to find more specific examples on the web and through other resources such as blogs, conferences, and online courses. Adoption within your industry will give you some idea of the potential for success, but if there is little adoption evident, don't be put off. This could indicate simply that you are ahead of the industry in thinking about this.

8. Are you in a highly regulated industry, such as financial services or pharmaceuticals, in which extra caution is required in your communications programs?

   Your company's industry and marketplace may make it more or less conducive to social media programs. Certain industries will have limits to the kind of communications programs in which a company could comfortably participate. For example, privacy and regulatory concerns might limit companies in financial services, stock and commodities trading, healthcare, legal, government agencies, and some other industries.

   In most cases, these limitations will not entirely preclude participation in social media programs but will be a factor in your social media strategy and may require additional layers of oversight and review. To better understand this in the context of your company's specific situation, you should work closely with your legal and finance departments to understand, and respond to, any concerns they might have.

Business Objectives

9. Would your company benefit from more cross-functional team collaboration?

   One of the benefits of internal social media programs is improvement of cross-functional collaboration. Internal blogs, communities, and other social media can provide employees and management with a new level of engagement and intimacy in their communications. As this should be a goal in any company, it is one area in which you can clearly "sell" social media and its benefits within the company.

10. Do you use the results of focus groups, surveys, and other customer data to make changes to your products, processes, and policies?

A company that uses focus groups, surveys, market research, and other information sources to influence its business is one that is willing to look outside its walls for information to guide the company on new product and service introductions, new ways of providing customer support, and the company's leadership position in the marketplace.

Many forms of social media offer the company the next generation of customer data, so a company with an established willingness to invest in collecting this data, and a commitment to responding to such information, will better see the potential for social media in this context.

11. Does your management evaluate the success of your communications initiatives solely on traditional business metrics, like revenue and margin?

Depending on your company's financial health, executive leadership, and culture, there may be specific, preferred methods for measuring the success of communications initiatives. This is important since social media measurement is an emerging field, and you may be unable to show direct correlation between your social media programs and revenue generation and margin, for example. You *will* be able to show things like additional site traffic and improved brand awareness.

As you design your social media programs, you obviously need to develop a strategy for measuring effectiveness to the satisfaction of your management. Most likely you will have to persuade them that "softer" measures like engagement and brand awareness are important to the company, so you should be prepared to do that when you present your social media strategy.

Engagement

12. Do you actively monitor what's being "said" about the company through traditional channels, such as print media?

13. Do you actively monitor what's being "said" about the company through Web 2.0/social media channels, such as blogs, social networks, and online communities?

Most large companies have both internal public relations organizations, and agency support for monitoring the effectiveness of their media relations programs. Typical of these is the "coverage report," outlining external responses to the company's activities such as press coverage and other "mentions" in the media. These are often qualified simply as positive, negative, or neutral, or they may be subject to more sophisticated analysis in which things like company messaging and competitive factors are considered.

This same kind of monitoring is easily done in the world of social media. It can be done either manually, via web search, or through the use of automated software tools designed for this purpose. (These are addressed in Chapter 3, "What are Social Media and Web 2.0?," in the section "Launching an Executive Blog.")

14. Do you respond to negative "buzz" about the company?

Another company attribute that will affect the company's effective participation in social media is its willingness to deal openly with negative comments and coverage. Sadly, some companies choose to ignore negative comments and hope they simply go away. Others see many discussions as isolated rants by angry consumers, not worthy of an "official" company response.

Many social media channels, such as blogs (both internal and external), Twitter, and customer communities offer the company numerous opportunities to respond to criticism in a highly effective manner and turn a seemingly bad situation to its advantage.

For example, if a blogger writes a negative post about a product, the manufacturer could either ignore it, thereby leaving the negative information as-is for anyone to find through a web search on the company's name, or a company representative could leave an objective, explanatory response on the blog, correcting any misinformation, and thereby setting the record straight and regaining some control of the conversation.

15. Do your customers consider peer reviews or word of mouth in purchasing products like yours?

It's important to understand whether your customers rely on peer reviews and other forms of word-of-mouth communications in considering purchases of products and services in your industry. Many consumers use blogs, online user reviews, and other forms of social media to make purchasing decisions, and this naturally increases the potential for your company to use social media to influence these decisions.

For example, social media plays a strong role in the selection of technology products. There are both individual blogs and blog networks dedicated to topics like consumer electronics, small- and medium-sized businesses, and enterprise IT.

For consumer services businesses, online peer review rating sites like Yelp can be very influential in the buying process. In these scenarios, consumers place more credibility on the information offered by other independent consumers than they do on information from official company sources. A set of websites featuring peer review is available on Consumerreview.com, with specific sites for photographic equipment, golf, audio gear, bicycles, and other consumer products.

You should identify as many of the places as possible online where these kinds of conversations take place and then factor this in your social media strategy. Under the right circumstances, this could become a one of the richest, most rewarding channels for your company's customer communications.

Culture

16. Do your clients and customers currently use social media for business purposes?

   Another factor to evaluate when considering your company's readiness for social media is the extent to which your clients/customers and business partners are using social media. This will determine whether social media will have good adoption among these people, or if they are not truly social media savvy, whether they might require additional education and promotion or may be entirely unwilling to employ social media for certain communications tasks. The best way to research this is through a search of blogs and social networks, through market research, or perhaps by a company-initiated survey of these groups.

17. Are your employees active on Facebook, MySpace, or other social networks?

   This is difficult factor to assess. Many of your employees may already be active on Facebook, MySpace, and other social networks, and some will be extremely well-versed in social media. This is particularly true of younger employees. This is the proverbial double-edged sword within many companies that may recognize the value of having well-connected employees who understand the technology but may also be threatened by the perceived (or real) issues of productivity, reputation, and information security presented by employee use of external communications tools.

Whether this is a good thing or bad thing also depends on how they have been using these networks in the past. Employees who use Facebook, for example, strictly for personal activities, friendships, and socializing may have misconceptions about suitable external conduct and appropriate use of company time. On the plus side, they will have a daily working familiarity with the tools and a clear understanding of the power of social media, which will apply equally in a corporate setting.

If instead of predominantly personal or social use, employees have previously been using social networks like Facebook, LinkedIn, and Plaxo in a professional or career development capacity, this may be extremely useful in their development. Most people who become proficient in social networking develop a community of professionals with similar interests whom they can tap for information and referrals to other resources and whom they can influence in regards to perceptions about the company.

18. Does anyone within the company blog on business-related issues?

Even if you don't have an official company blog, your company may already have active bloggers writing on appropriate topics. These people can serve as the leads for some of your social media initiatives. For example, if one or more of the company's technical people already have a following on an independent blog, you might consider bringing that person and his or her blog into a more formal company blogging environment. Or, you could take steps so that the blog clearly identifies him or her as an employee and representative of the company, and you could link to and from the blog from the company's website. If the content of the blog is appropriate, this strategy can give you an almost instant entry into corporate social media.

19. Do any of your company's social media "experts" participate in external conferences on subjects like social media, corporate communications, or Web 2.0?

Just as your company may already have active bloggers, you may have people who are particularly well-versed in social media, and even recognized as industry experts, who currently speak at conferences and industry events. These people are valuable resources who can influence other professionals and can learn about and influence the direction of social media in general.

Competent participation in these conferences also serves to generate incredible goodwill for the company in the social media world. Like anything examined under the social media magnifying lens, the speakers, what they have to say, and their companies have the opportunity to become widely known among social media experts for their expertise. A good example of this is Dell, well known for their broad use of social media and supported by several highly visible social media evangelists who participate actively both online and in live conferences.

20. Does your company embrace less formal communication with the outside world without the involvement of the legal, marketing, and PR departments?

Another cultural measure of a company's potential for success in social media is its willingness to allow its employees and its leadership to participate in less formal communications with the outside world. For example, the very best executive blogs are those that are relevant, current, and frequently updated by the executive. These updates could come any time of day or night from anywhere in the world, and a company unwilling to trust its executives to communicate properly on behalf of the company will have too many reviews and processes to allow this kind of spontaneous communications.

In other areas of social media, like Twitter and other social networks, opportunities to speak on the company's behalf may occur in "real time." If employees feel they can represent the company without fear of retribution, they will be more apt to weigh in as goodwill ambassadors. Some companies have dozens or even hundreds of employees "carrying the message" through various forms of social media.

Hopefully, the SocialCorp Readiness Quiz and these explanations have helped you develop a broad perspective on the company's potential to adopt and take advantage of social media. As you read through the rest of the book, you'll come to understand the incredible power of corporate social media to influence the people you need to reach with your message. Many factors will affect your success, and you'll need the cooperation of numerous people and organizations within the company to successfully implement these programs.

What Are Social Media and Web 2.0?

A quick web search will yield dozens of definitions for the terms *social media* and *Web 2.0*. These were discussed earlier, but it's helpful to have additional context on how these tools and technologies can be best used in a corporate communications environment.

There is plenty of debate over the precise meaning of the term Web 2.0. Even Tim O'Reilly, generally acknowledged as the originator of the term, gives it a dual definition:

> "Web 2.0 is the business revolution in the computer industry caused by the move to the Internet as a platform, and an attempt to understand the rules for success on that new platform."

From a business standpoint, Web 2.0 can be seen as the next version of the Web. Web 2.0 is also a set of technologies that form the infrastructure on which this new web is deployed.

While this book is not a technical guide to the implementation of social media, especially given the complexity of many corporate IT environments, it is useful to understand social media and Web 2.0 within a basic technical framework in order to evaluate what is reasonable or possible within your company. Some companies, particularly larger ones with sophisticated IT, may find it difficult or impossible to implement certain social media tools.

This chapter will provide an overview of the more popular social media tools in use in corporate communications, and it will offer a few examples of companies using the tools. Later chapters will provide more in-depth examples.

Choosing the Right Social Media Tools

As previously mentioned, social media strategy should tie to business and communication strategy, rather than being based on the available tools. But it is not possible to develop a social media strategy without at least having an understanding of the various tools that are available, their functionality and purposes, and the kinds of audiences and conversations for which they might be best suited.

There are many different categories and types of social media that might be useful in a corporation. Most familiar are publicly available consumer-grade social media applications such as social networks like Facebook and MySpace, microblogging sites like Twitter and Pownce, video posting and sharing sites like YouTube and Blip.TV, and social bookmarking sites like Digg and Delicious. Publicly available social media has its advantages. Many have tens of millions of users, providing companies with instant access to large, specific demographic groups of interest. They are also generally free of charge, funded through contextual advertising. This "free" business model has both benefits and drawbacks in a corporate environment.

Considering the Free Options

Arguments in favor of using free, publicly available consumer style social media tools are many. For example, a social network like Facebook or MySpace, or a community built on a platform like Ning, already has infrastructure in place and requires no software development by the corporation. The companies that own these sites take responsibility for hosting, storage, data management, backup, security, user identity management, and all of the other IT tasks associated with running a social media site. The potential downside to this approach is that the corporation cannot maintain control over the quality of the IT environment. The microblogging service Twitter, for example, has been plagued by inadequate and poorly architected IT, making an incredibly innovative tool frustrating, difficult to use, and of questionable value for serious business communications. Twitter has shown some improvement, with users widely acknowledging Twitter's outstanding performance on election night, November 4, 2008.

Another concern regarding the use of public social media is security. In most cases effective use of consumer social media will be limited to communications activities that are intended for external audiences. It is unlikely that Facebook or Twitter would be used for the distribution of any sensitive information. This is not true, of course, in the case of certain collaboration tools like wikis and other social media specifically designed to accommodate the security requirements of internal communications.

Copyright, license, and ownership of content should be considered when using public social media. Before adopting a particular tool, you should review its terms of service and user agreement to fully understand who owns the content posted on the social media site. In many cases the licenses to use these sites require the user to authorize other public use and reuse of some information.

Finally, as previously mentioned, the so-called "free" business model means that your audience will generally be subject to contextual advertising. While most consumers have become accustomed to daily bombardment with advertising messages, there is still a risk to the corporation that its social media communications will be positioned next to inappropriate advertising content, whether because that content touches on subjects the company does not wish its brand to be associated with, or which, in some cases, could direct consumers to a competitive company or product. Arguably, in a free market economy, a company's products and services should win out on their real value to consumers and businesses, but it is simply not smart to help potential customers identify and purchase competitive products.

Playing Together Nicely

Another interesting aspect in the selection of appropriate social media tools is that in many cases they work quite well together despite being offered by independent companies. So, for example, if you choose to post all your images on Flickr, not only will Flickr provide an environment for hosting and tagging those images, but Flickr users are in and of themselves an additional community that is now within your reach. Many will post your Flickr images to other sites, creating a network of links back to your company. This is the web in action, with each connection or discrete set of connections branching out to another set of connections, quickly and exponentially increasing the reach of your communications.

Social Media Applications for Corporate Communications

The previous section mentioned the various categories and grades of social media tools and the publicly available consumer sites and services. There are several other categories, each with its own unique characteristics and considerations for adoption in a corporate environment. Within the consumer class of social media, there are sometimes multiple subscription or user levels available, so that additional features and functionality can be purchased on top of the basic no-cost functionality of the entry-level consumer products. This is particularly true with wiki and collaboration tools.

A class of social media tools that this book will not cover is that of widgets, plug-ins and add-ons. These include small programs, utilities, and pieces of software code that extend and enhance the functionality of existing social media tools or interconnect the input and output of various tools.

Enterprise Grade Social Media

Of great interest in a corporate environment are a relatively new class of social media tools that can be considered enterprise grade. While once the domain of web pioneers and early adopters, social media has reached critical mass, and corporate users are demanding social media applications and infrastructure built to the same enterprise standards as the customer relationship management, e-commerce, human resources, and other applications offered by large, established vendors like Oracle, IBM, and SAP.

Larger software providers have seen the market for enterprise-grade corporate social media. Most of the major industry analyst firms, like Forrester and Gartner, have launched social media or social software practices and assigned analysts to cover companies and products in the market.

In addition to looking at social software available from traditional software vendors, many companies either not finding the functionality they want in publicly available social media or wishing to maintain more control, are developing their own tools and infrastructure. Pfizer, for example, has created an internal social network code-named Pfacebook. IBM created its own version of microblogging environment Twitter, nicknaming it Blue Twit.

Another aspect of social media that is both a blessing and a curse is that application development can often be done quickly using application programming interfaces (APIs), simplified connections to existing tools, and development environments like Ruby on Rails and other technology for quick prototyping and development. This means that social media applications can often be created and deployed very quickly, and almost any entrepreneur with a good (or not so good) idea can get "in the game." It also means that applications can be developed without consideration for long-term factors like scale (the ability to grow to accommodate millions or tens of millions of users) or integration with an enterprise environment. The classic case study on this is Twitter, which in early 2008 was plagued for many months with downtime, "broken" features, and other problems due to poorly architected IT.

That's Not How You Spell "Digg"

As you have probably observed, the field is dominated by silly sounding names. Advances in social media often come from technical people who are well known for coining fanciful product names. Social media is quite often created by younger entrepreneurs, and unusual naming conventions, graphic design, and even business models are a rebellion against the image of stodgy corporate software vendors.

Another factor is the lack of availability of simple, English language domains, like ask.com. This has forced companies to use alternate spellings for what sound like regular words, like Flickr, Digg, and Yoono, and to coin entirely new words like Plurk and Jaiku.

Blogs

The original social media breakthrough occurred with the introduction of the *blog*, a word combining *web* and *log*. The original blogs were generally text-only, supplemented by a few still images, and were daily logs of the blogger's life activities. Like chat (instant messaging) before them, much of the early blog content was highly trivial in nature, and only later did blogs mature and become focused on specific topics like information technology and entertainment. Today, anyone can blog. Technorati (a blog search and ranking site) indexes about 140 million blogs, with about a third in English.

Simply put, a blog is a live website that any user can edit quickly with little or no technical skill. Blog articles are called *posts*, and they are generally, but not always, no more than 1000 words in length, usually much less. A blog post can include regular text (with some formatting like bold, italic, and bulleted lists), still images, links to other blogs, and even embedded video and Flash animations.

The magic of the blog happens the moment the blogger finishes writing a post and clicks the publish button. The blogging software "pings" the blogosphere (all of the blog search sites, news readers, and so on) and notifies the world that new content has been posted. In this way, the newly posted information is made instantly available to millions of people around the globe.

Blogging has evolved into a highly complex and very popular medium, with many bloggers having widespread influence on a scale previously afforded only to high-profile broadcast and print journalists.

Like almost all social media, blogs can be deployed in any number of ways. Popular blogging platforms include WordPress, Movable Type, Blogger, and TypePad. (Most of these applications are available online, often at no charge.) Within each of these platforms, deployment can generally be done in one of three ways. WordPress, for example, allows users to establish a blog at wordpress.com, to create a WordPress blog hosted by an independent hosting company, or to install WordPress on their own servers.

There are many kinds of blogs a company could deploy, such as an executive blog in which the CEO and or other senior executives of the company publish regular posts. One of the best known CEO blogs is written by Jonathan Schwartz, CEO of Sun Microsystems (**Figure 3.1**). Jonathan is a pioneer among senior executive bloggers and writes a thoughtful and widely followed blog.

Figure 3.1
*Jonathan Schwartz
blog home page.*

Blogging has not caught on widely at the senior-most levels of most companies for several reasons. Later chapters will go into detail on some of the reasons, but principally, these involve perceived risk, priorities, and lack of executive time. In a corporate environment, particularly in a publicly held company, allowing senior executives free access to use the company's public website to post their personal commentary and thoughts may seem too risky for some corporate communicators. The typical executive at any level of the company already faces intense time pressure and in many cases is unwilling to set aside the time to maintain a blog.

While CEO blogs gain the most attention, it's not always practical or appropriate for the CEO to maintain a blog. There are many other types of blogs, such as the group blog, that are also effective. A *group blog* could be comprised of several executives at various levels within the company posting to the blog on a regular basis on one or more topics. These topics could, but do not have to, relate directly to the company's products and markets, or could simply be a set of leadership themes that help articulate the company's strategy and market leadership. Bloggers need not be drawn from the senior executive ranks of the company. Almost any articulate person, with experience and expertise on an important topic, writing ability, and the time to update the blog on a regular basis is a candidate for a company group blog.

Most blogs offer commenting, which allows visitors to the blog to leave comments on a particular post. The ability to leave comments is one of the many conversational or participatory elements of social media. Commenting is symbolic of the sweeping changes social media is bringing to the corporate world. For the first time, anyone with access to a web browser can post nearly anything they'd like to say directly to a company's website. This can be a challenge to communications professionals, who may fear losing control of the company's "message," or might simply be concerned about inappropriate content in a comment. Comments can be moderated, which means they are held in a queue for an editor to approve prior to posting. Profanity and other inappropriate content can also be caught by spam filters.

While most industry attention centers around external blogs as tools for reaching customers, influential bloggers, and the media, many companies use internal blogs for a number of purposes, including leadership communications, sharing of best practices within engineering and product development communities, and as a way to give all employees a voice within the company.

Sun Microsystems, for example, permits nearly any employee with an interest in blogging to do so and allows those blogs to be linked publicly.

Hewlett-Packard has a large group blog with authorized company spokes-people blogging on various products and topics. HP also provides links to employee-written blogs of all kinds, many of which are simply a reflection of the employee's personal interests and hobbies and aren't related to their employment at the company.

For more suggestions on corporate blogging, see the section "Launching an Executive Blog."

 If your executives are reluctant to commit the time necessary for blogging, have them compose their blog posts in an email and send them to corporate communications for posting. This will save them time, allow them to use email (a medium with which they are no doubt already comfortable), make the process less formal, and free them from having to learn how to use the blogging software.

Social Networks

Perhaps the best known and most widely used social media tools are social networks like MySpace, Facebook, and LinkedIn. Twitter, often called a microblogging environment, has some characteristics of a social network but is an unusual hybrid, which we'll discuss later.

The idea of the social network is that users create a profile and then add friends, contacts, connections, and so on. (There are many different terms for these depending on the network.) They either already know these people through work or other associations or have similar interests and background. Trust, based on prior association and transparency, is the backbone of the social network.

Some networks are used for business and professional reasons; others are for personal and leisure use. However, with competition, and the growing number of subscribers each network has to serve, the lines between the types of networks and reasons for choosing one over another are blurring.

Recruiters and candidates often meet on LinkedIn. Plaxo Pulse is aimed at the person who is in an established career. Facebook, created for college and university users, was opened to everyone in 2007 and now boasts about 100 million users. MySpace, once the domain of under-30s, has seen steady user growth and a rising age demographic, and, according to one report, about 40 percent of users are now 35 or older.

Social networking is now mainstream, with two out of every three Internet users regularly visiting a social networking site. According to Comscore, "The number of worldwide visitors to social networking sites has grown 34 percent in the past year to 530 million." In some regions, such as the UK, social networking sites account for more than 75 percent of all web traffic.

FACEBOOK

Facebook has become quite popular with corporations as a means of reaching certain demographic groups inexpensively and in a way that is comfortable for them. This is typical of another aspect of social media that is new to corporate communicators. The company website is no longer the center of the communications universe. An effective social media strategy involves knowing how to reach people where they live, work, and play instead of expecting them to come to you.

Companies can use Facebook by creating a *group* or *page*. Typically these groups and pages are designed to support a particular initiative or purpose rather than serve a broader, companywide purpose.

Ernst and Young became the first company to launch a company-sponsored Facebook page to recruit college students. Ernst and Young used the page to share information about the company's culture and to describe the application process. Ernst and Young's employees answer candidate questions personally on the page, enabling students to connect with the company in a more intimate and relevant way.

BMW used Facebook (**Figure 3.2**) to launch the BMW 1-Series, a compact coupe and convertible. The car's smaller size is a deviation from BMW's traditional sizing standards. The company launched a Graffiti Car Contest on Facebook to convince potential customers that the new I-Series is in line with BMW's brand despite being smaller and less expensive than other series. The Graffiti Car Contest hosted on Facebook received more than 9,000 submissions within the first seven days. Facebook users designed virtual cars and shared them with friends. The contest led to buzz in the blogosphere and was reported on by *The New York Times*.

> **IDEA** Create a Facebook page to generate interest in the launch of a new product. You can support this with contextual advertising within Facebook, promotions, or by creating a fun viral application like a trivia quiz or game thematically tied to the page to generate additional interest.

Figure 3.2
BMW *Facebook page.*

PHOTO SHARING

While adding an image directly to a blog post is one way to share photos online, there are advantages to using a popular photo sharing service like Flickr. Once a photo is on a site like Flickr, you can add it to a blog post with a few clicks.

With Flickr, you establish an account and upload pictures either from your computer desktop or from your digital camera or mobile phone. Flickr allows you to title and describe each picture and tag it with keywords and descriptions so that it can be found in an image search. Some people—photographers, graphic artists, and those with portfolios, for example—don't maintain a regular blog and just use Flickr to store and share photos. Like many photo sites, Flickr also enables online ordering for prints. Flickr also allows you to edit photos online using its picnik editing tool.

In addition to maintaining a blog, GM has decided to share high-quality photos on Flickr. On GM's Flickr account you will find calendars featuring GM cars, photos from press events, and images of a wide range of car models. With over a thousand images posted, GM has made a sustained commitment to its presence on Flickr that goes beyond the *campaign* mentality that sometimes pervades marketing and public relations.

IDEA Use Flickr for posting images and video during live coverage of a company event. You can create an embedded Flickr feed, such that the images and video can appear almost instantly on your website, blog, or digital newsroom.

COMMUNITIES

A community shares many characteristics with a blog, but is designed to accommodate larger numbers of participants in a slightly different manner. While blogs are normally organized along chronological and categorical lines by blog post, communities are organized by topic or forum. Communities are usually dedicated to those with a common interest, such as public relations professionals, readers of mystery novels, or members of a particular club or organization.

Unlike traditional websites, community management is usually decentralized, with control and responsibility for upkeep divided among a handful of dedicated, inspired (and often unpaid) members who manage the community out of passion for its members and its mission.

Popular community building applications include Ning, KickApps, and CrowdVine.

The IT company Symantec created the Symantec Technology Network (STN) discussion forums (**Figure 3.3**) to engage more closely with customers. STN has thousands of participants and has generated tens of thousands of discussion comments, demonstrating the power of some social media to enable a company to take advantage of the passion and knowledge of its customers.

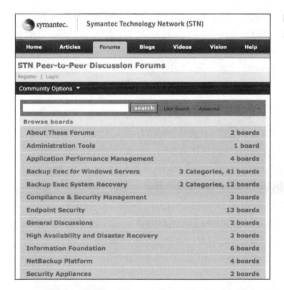

Figure 3.3 *Symantec Technology Network discussion forum.*

Research in Motion (RIM,) best known for the BlackBerry phone, has created the BlackBerry Owner's Lounge, a community for its customers. In the Lounge, BlackBerry owners can voice their opinions through interactive polls, download productivity and game content, and connect with other BlackBerry members. These features give owners more ways to use their BlackBerry phones, building brand loyalty and improving customer satisfaction.

Social Bookmarking

You may have noticed the small icons at the bottom of some blog posts with names like Digg, Delicious, and StumbleUpon. These are links to social bookmarking sites.

Social bookmarking is similar to the bookmarking function available through your web browser. With one click, you can mark a blog or an article as a "favorite." Like all social media, the difference with social bookmarking is the social aspect—your bookmarks are available to everyone on the web. The bookmarking site then rates each item on popularity, based on the number of times it was bookmarked.

Bookmarking is part of the highly elaborate social media popularity contest. The more links that lead to a particular blog or blog post, the higher its *authority* rating with Google Blog Search, Technorati, and other blog search tools. Blogs with higher authority appear higher up in search results.

Like a traditional website, the value of a social media site to a sponsor is based on its traffic. Better search results translate into better traffic. On a social bookmarking site like Digg, the more people who bookmarked a particular item, the higher it appears on the page in search results, generating more traffic to the blog, and so on. Until you really dig in (no social bookmarking pun intended) and start using these tools, it's hard to understand all of the implications.

There are dozens of social bookmarking tools, and each behaves a little differently. One of the most popular is Digg. Here's how it works. Once you're signed up for Digg, you can Digg an item (add it to your favorites, thereby giving it what is called "a Digg" or "Digging it" as in **Figure 3.4**). You can log into your account and either click a Digg This icon at the bottom of the item you are interested in, or if there is no icon on the page, copy the URL (web location) from your browser and paste it into your page on Digg. From there you can add a comment, and if you have a blog, you also have the option to post the item to your blog. You can go to the Digg home page (www.digg.com) to see the latest popular items.

Figure 3.4 *Digg it on diggs.*

Digg, with its connections to search and ranking and its ability to integrate with your blog, is just one of many examples of how independent social media tools interoperate with each other to broaden your communications reach.

Social bookmarking capability is something that should be incorporated in all your social media initiatives. It's also useful for you as you read various blogs and websites and wish to capture links to information you find interesting or helpful.

An equally important use of social bookmarking is for bloggers and journalists who visit your external sites and find an item they wish to share with their readers or wish to refer to on their blogs. In many cases the social bookmarking service automates this process. Digg, for example, allows you to not only Digg (bookmark) an item, but with a few more clicks of the mouse, you can enter a few comments and then post the item to your blog. Google reader behaves similarly, allowing users to quickly post links to the reader and then automatically to a blog.

Rich Media

Clearly, one of the biggest changes brought about by the social media revolution is in the proliferation of video. The convergence of inexpensive web cams (in some cases built in to PCs), free/inexpensive video editing software, and free online services for posting, sharing, and viewing video has driven the creation of millions of hours of user-generated video content now available online.

There are many popular video upload sites and a number of different ways of managing video content.

YouTube: The Original Online Video Site

The most well-known online video site is YouTube, now owned by Google. YouTube is a popular site for uploading videos and allowing people to share and comment on them. Not only are people making personalized videos of their life experiences, but businesses are making use of YouTube as well, posting TV commercials, humorous videos, instructional material, video archives of executive speeches, and so on.

YouTube is archival, and it's largely one-way in that a user records the video and posts it. It's not engaged in a live, two-way conversation, although viewers may rate the video and leave comments on the YouTube site.

The YouTube player—the onscreen video box with the stop/play and volume controls—can be embedded easily into any blog or community by copying a short line of code from the player itself into a blog. Each player has a slightly different way of doing this, and each blogging tool also has its own procedure, but it's not hard to do. Embedded videos are a popular blog and community feature.

Two other kinds of services have since emerged that have built on the social video metaphor: streaming video and video chat. There are many tools available in both categories, but let's look at two of the most popular.

Ustream.TV: Streaming Internet Video

Unlike YouTube, which only permits posting of finished video content, Ustream and similar services allow users to create their own Internet broadcast channels and programs, through which they can stream live video. There are still bandwidth and encoding issues to overcome, so video quality is not what you would expect from your home entertainment system, but it is generally more than adequate for business, instructional, and news and analysis content. Ustream users have streamed weddings, births, seminars, concerts, celebrity interviews, and many other kinds of personal and business-related programming. For in-house use, Ustream channels can be password-protected so that only authorized viewers can access them. There is also a chat room option, so that viewers can comment and ask questions during the video stream.

Seesmic: Internet Video Chat

The Seesmic video metaphor falls somewhere between that of YouTube and Ustream. Seesmic users record short video clips and upload them to the site. Each clip serves as the basis for a *thread*, a related series of streams. By clicking a thread, you can watch, in chronological order (or not), all of the videos on a topic so that you see an entire conversation, albeit one made of short snippets of video.

These kinds of services offer an interesting and sometimes awkward hybrid of personal communications and media. The people creating the videos may regard them as informal interpersonal communications, but "viewers" can be more critical, evaluating videos against professionally produced blockbuster movies, resulting in unreasonable expectations of quality.

Other Internet Video Chat Applications

A service similar to Seesmic, called Utterli (get used to it, Web 2.0 names can be downright silly) allows users to phone in an Utter (an audio post) from their cell phones. It's very handy for posting random thoughts from anywhere in the world, without a computer, or even a keyboard. Content uploaded to Seesmic, Utterli, and other online audio and video sites can also be manually embedded in a blog, or in some cases, the service can be configured to do this automatically.

Another interesting emerging video application is cell phone streaming video. Services like Qik allow users to stream live video from anywhere they can obtain a cellular connection. Like other archival and streaming video services, mobile phone-based video services allow for embedding a video player on a blog, company website, and so on. While not offering perhaps the best resolution for streaming video, this is an interesting application and can be useful for event coverage, "man on the street" reporting, and other breaking coverage.

Enterprise-Grade Video

There are many companies now offering enterprise-grade social media–enabled video solutions. These companies offer a video player similar in appearance and functionality to the YouTube video player and offer several options in relation to size and appearance. The player can be customized to match the company's website color scheme and branding, and can incorporate the company's logo. While the player is just the "front end" of the system, a branded player can be a highly effective component of your social media strategy. It has a more professional appearance than a generic third-party player and therefore integrates easily with the company's existing online vehicles. Behind this so-called front end is video hosting, also offered by many of the companies that provide the players. Streaming video hosting can be tricky, particularly when surges in viewing occur during widely publicized events, like quarterly earnings calls, and similar situations. Many streaming video hosting companies have good experience managing wildly fluctuating workloads, and they have the infrastructure and bandwidth to guarantee that visitors to your site will be able to access the video when they want to.

There are a number of companies offering these services. Brightcove is quite popular, and was selected by Seagate for its Digital Newsroom. GM's corporate site hosts its videos with The Feedroom. Sun Microsystems, a pioneer in online video for corporate communications and marketing, uses both The Feedroom and Akamai Streamos.

Video player licensing and streaming video hosting costs vary depending upon the provider; they're sometimes based on the size and number of videos streamed. It's important to understand the business model of whatever video hosting company you choose. Some of these are pure production and hosting companies. Others aspire to being media companies or video networks. Similar to the issues presented by the free upload services, the network model might affect positioning of your message, so it is worth investigating.

 Implement a quarterly video news segment for internal distribution. Have a senior executive act as the host, interviewing other company executives, engineers, marketing and sales people, and customers. Video content is light and highly engaging and will help your company leadership engage with employees on a more intimate and effective basis.

What's the Buzz Out There?

With over 100 million blogs, several hundred thousand news sites, and at least 50 online wire services cranking out press releases, how is it possible for you or your audience to find and read everything of interest? It's not. Leave it to Web 2.0 to offer at least a dozen solutions to this problem. An understanding of blog search alerts, RSS (really simple syndication), and news readers and aggregators will help you understand how people will find and read your company news, while at the same time giving you the tools to research what others are saying about you and your company, your competition, and your marketplace.

Blog Search

The best way to find new blogs to read, if you're starting from scratch, is to do a blog search. This is generally not the same thing as a traditional web search. The best tools for this are Technorati and Google Blog Search. If you are looking for blogs to enhance your professional life, use one of these services to search on work-related terms, like your company name or product names. Search on the name of your profession and on your job title. Once you find interesting blogs, you can bookmark them in your browser, or if you have your own blog, add them to the blogroll (a list of blogs you read).

Eventually, you may want to automate the blog reading process, rather than clicking a link and physically visiting every blog on your list on a regular basis. You can do this through alerts and RSS feeds.

Alerts

Google offers a really useful tool, called an *alert*, that allows you to receive an email notification when a certain blog is updated or when new information on a given topic is published somewhere. Setting one up is simple. Just find a search that works, such as *3G phones*, and then click the Alert link on the left side of the screen. You can set your alert to notify you immediately any time there is an update, or you can elect to have a daily summary email sent to you.

RSS and Newsreaders

Another way to receive regular blog updates is through an RSS feed. An RSS feed is a universal format for exchanging content between social media sites. Via RSS, news can be delivered to a standalone desktop newsreader, a newsreader built into the web browser, or even sent to the user's cell phone.

RSS has many applications in corporate social media. It can be used, for example, to display on the company's website summaries of the latest posts from the company's blog. RSS feeds can also be used to display blog posts and similar content for internal audiences on the company's intranet sites. A comprehensive social media strategy should always include employees, and often there is social media content being created elsewhere on the company's blog, newsroom, and so on that would be interesting and relevant to employees. RSS allows the company to rebroadcast this information instantly and at no cost to other social media vehicles within the company.

Nearly all blogs include RSS feeds, which can be accessed either through a link with the label *RSS* or *Feed*, or sometimes through a small orange icon (**Figure 3.5**) indicating the availability of a feed.

Some of the more popular newsreaders include standalone readers like Bloglines or NetNewsWire, or they can be part of a larger environment, such as Google News Reader.

Figure 3.5
RSS icon indicating availability of a feed.

Set up **RSS** feeds on your blogs and websites by categories that are most useful to your audience. For example, if you are a storage company, certain industry analysts may be interested only in your computer consumer products, whereas others may be following the enterprise storage industry. Securities analysts may only be interested in financial reporting. If you establish RSS feeds based on these categories, they will be most useful to the people you are trying to reach and therefore more likely to be adopted and used on a regular basis.

 Keep your corporate communications team informed of breaking news about your company. Establish RSS feeds based on keywords such as your company name, product names, and the names of competitors and their products, and create a Yahoo alert that can transmit any newly published news items on these topics directly to your team members' cell phones.

Emerging Social Media

In addition to the applications mentioned previously, there are forms of social media that are less widely known but are also worth consideration in a corporate communications environment.

Each of these applications subtly changes the established social media metaphor. *Microblogging*, for example, is a hybrid of blogging, instant messaging, chat, and a news feed, and generally limits each text-only post (aka *update*) to a certain number of characters, in most cases 140 to 160.

Wikis are extremely popular for internal collaboration and project management, and in many ways are the social media equivalent of Microsoft's SharePoint and other enterprise collaboration technology.

And finally, 3-D virtual worlds like Linden Lab's Second Life and Google's Lively offer corporations an interesting albeit somewhat unusual medium for communications.

Twitter: Microblogging

Twitter is the latest, hottest thing in social media. It's hard to understand the tremendous appeal and usefulness of Twitter until you have been using it for a while. It's part of a new class of blogging platforms called microblogging, with limited feature sets and simplified functionality as compared to traditional blogs, but it's so much more than that. Twitter is a social network, a community, a chat, an intelligently moderated news feed, and anything else you want it to be.

Once you're signed up for Twitter, which takes about three minutes, you can post 140-character updates (also known as *tweets*—I told you Web 2.0 names were silly) for all the world to see. Images and formatting are not permitted, though links are allowed. You get just 140 characters to express yourself (**Figure 3.6**). You can add connections (friends and colleagues) on Twitter, called *followers*.

Figure 3.6 *Tweets on a Twitter page.*

What's amazing is all of the things people have figured out they can do with Twitter. Whether intentionally or through divine intervention, Twitter got everything "right." Some people use Twitter like a chat room. Others use it like a social network. As I mentioned, images and formatting are not permitted, but links are, so Twitter can also be useful as a moderated news feed. (You see only selected links published by your friends, so you have smart people with similar interests sharing links.)

Businesses are flocking to Twitter. Corporations that use Twitter, generally for reaching consumers, come from a wide range of industries including retail, travel, and automotive. Computer manufacturer Dell is well-known for its early and quite effective presence on Twitter, and the company not only provides product support and engages with customers on Twitter, but claims to have generated a half million dollars through Twitter.

Other companies on Twitter include Carnival Cruise Lines, *Harpers* magazine, Popeyes Chicken, and JetBlue.

While Twitter is part of this new wave of microblogging environments, *bite-sized blogs*, if you will, like Jaiku, Pownce, and possibly Tumblr, it is a "breakout hit" and a phenomenon that defies classification. Dave Winer, a well-known blogger, likened Twitter to "the next DNS (Domain Name System)," suggesting that its influence and importance will become global and all-encompassing.

With all its praises, Twitter also has its problems. The service is notorious for interruptions and downtime, making it of questionable value for serious business use, although much progress has been made in correcting this. There are also consumer trust issues on Twitter. Like all online services, Twitter has its Terms of Service (TOS) posted on its site, a list of rules to which all users must agree, but the company has been accused of failing to strictly enforce them. There have been numerous incidents of Twitter users falsely representing themselves or well-known companies.

In August 2008, social media experts applauded ExxonMobil for its venture on Twitter, when a new user called ExxonMobilCorp signed up for the service. Unfortunately, after investigation by Forrester analyst and blogger Jeremiah Owyang, it turned out that Janet (the name of the person associated with the ExxonMobilCorp Twitter account) was not an authorized representative of the company.

While Twitter has some obligations to police this kind of activity, companies also need to monitor use of their name and identity across all social media to locate renegade communications activity and make a decision on how to handle it.

We'll look a little deeper at the issue of brand control and of ethical company representation in Chapter 4, "Can You Control Your Brand or Just Share It?" and Chapter 6, "Balancing Social Media Risk and Reward." For more information, see the sidebar "Twitter: Simple, Versatile Corporate Communications Tool."

Wikis

A wiki is an easily updated website with controls over various levels of users who range from readers who may only read the content on the wiki, to editors who can change the content, to administrators who can authorize new users, modify the appearance of the site, and enable and disable features. The name *wiki* was coined by Ward Cunningham to describe a website that is created and maintained by a group of editors and can be updated and modified quickly. Wiki comes from the Hawaiian phrase *wiki wiki*, which means quickly. (If you've been to a Hawaiian airport you may have seen the Wiki Wiki buses.)

The mother of all wikis is the widely known Wikipedia. Wikipedia is built on the Wikimedia platform, an open-source wiki solution. A close look at Wikipedia will give you a good idea of how a wiki works. You can see as you look at various Wikipedia entries the various stages of editing and content development. Some documents have achieved page status, which means the entries are complete and have been accepted by Wikipedia's editors. Others are referred to as *stubs*, which are pages in progress. While these terms are not always used in wikis outside of Wikipedia, they give you an idea of how a wiki is used to create "living" documents. There is a change audit trail for every Wikipedia entry, and behind every page are discussions on the content of that page so that anyone who wishes to gain more context into the thinking behind the final entry or would like to question inclusions or changes can see who is responsible for the content.

This kind of functionality makes a wiki ideal for many corporate applications. Wikis are popular for enterprise collaboration and are often used in applications where companies might also use Microsoft SharePoint. Popular wiki applications include project and event management, document version control, and for companywide manuals, policies and procedures, and style guides.

Perhaps the best-known vendor of enterprise-grade wiki software is Socialtext, a social media pioneer. There are many other options available to companies that wish to deploy wikis, including free public social media versions such as WetPaint, PBwiki, and Jotspot, which is now part of Google. (In fact, much of the research for this book was managed through a PBwiki.)

Second Life: Virtual Worlds

Another area that has been interesting to watch, yet slow to mature, is the use of Second Life and other virtual worlds as corporate communications tools. Second Life is an animated, 3D, virtual reality environment, populated by people who are represented by *avatars*, computer-generated characters, who may or may not look like the person behind them. Second Life was developed by Linden Labs, and within the Second Life environment, people buy and sell products, hold jobs, socialize, and do most of the things they could do in the real world. There is even a currency called Linden Bucks.

Many companies have tried establishing outposts on Second Life, but there is still doubt as to either its effectiveness from a communication standpoint or its ability to generate sustained revenue. IBM was an early Second Life participant. Other companies who have been on Second Life include Intel, Adidas, BMW, Sears, Sony Ericsson, Sprint, and Starwood Hotels.

A recent entry into the virtual world field is Google's new Lively environment. It is too soon to tell whether Lively will emerge as an effective corporate communications tool.

Twitter: Simple, Versatile Corporate Communications Tool

Hundreds of companies in a wide array of industries and markets, such as media, information technology, automotive, hospitality, air travel, apparel, and financial services, have created accounts on the microblogging site Twitter and are engaging one-to-one with consumers using a variety of communications models.

Among the Fortune 1000, Twitter is proving useful for customer support and customer service as well as general marketing communications and public relations.

Benefits include improved customer service and satisfaction; direct engagement with consumers; improved perception of the company and its brand; and positive coverage in the mainstream media for companies willing to do business in the public eye. To be successful on Twitter, companies need to understand the types of communications best suited to the medium; how to staff their Twitter accounts with appropriate personnel; when Twitter may not be the right choice; and how to set reasonable expectations for results.

As mentioned elsewhere in the book, Twitter has been characterized as a *microblogging* tool, but it's really much more than that. The "micro" designation refers to limits on length and type of supported content. Twitter updates can be no more than 140 characters of unformatted text, and links are permitted, but there's no way to include images or streaming content. This would seem limiting, but there are ways to "add" this functionality to Twitter, and the character limit forces communicators to be terse and efficient, which helps readers immensely.

Twitter's interface (**Figure 3.7**) allows users to convey quite a lot of information in a small space:

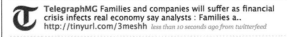

Figure 3.7
Twitter update.

In this example of a Twitter "tweet" (update), London's Telegraph Media Group is promoting a news item on the Telegraph website. The logo and TelegraphMG "handle" (user ID) let users know who the update came from. A user can click on the user ID to see the company's Twitter profile page. The tweet includes a brief summary of the news item and a link that has been shortened to fit the space using tinyurl.com. (In some cases Twitter automatically shortens URLs "on the fly.")

There is also a timestamp, which tells you how long ago recent entries were posted and provides a date and time for older entries. The timestamp also tells you where the update came from—Twitterfeed in this case, which automatically posts Twitter updates from a blog's RSS feed. There are also hidden buttons to bookmark this tweet as a favorite or to reply directly to it; the buttons appear when the user moves the mouse over the tweet.

Twitter has over three million registered users. Information posted on Twitter reaches an extended audience via its own support for SMS (texting by cell phone), instant messaging, and mobile clients (special "lightweight" versions of the Twitter application designed specifically for mobile phones), and through its API (application programming interface), which allows third parties to develop applications that access a user's data. Thanks to the API, Twitter is supported by hundreds of third-party services like Twitpic (image posting), Friendfeed (a social network activity aggregator), and Facebook (where Twitter updates can be automatically posted as Facebook status updates.) Third-party mobile clients are also available, including support for BlackBerry and iPhone.

Hundreds of companies have a presence on Twitter. GM, jetBlue, Zappos, Popeyes Chicken, Dell, *The New York Times*, Home Depot, Starbucks, and Bigelow Tea are among the growing list of companies using Twitter to engage with consumers.

The "Conversation Thing" is Real on Twitter

Twitter is the "online conversation" concept made real for corporations. In 2000, the authors of *The Cluetrain Manifesto* identified the global *conversations* taking place on the Internet and the need for companies to join in and make a positive contribution. Although this may seem like an abstract concept, it is an important one, and companies need to understand how to use Twitter to leverage this dynamic.

Companies with a presence on Twitter will be able to better *listen* to what consumers are saying about them and to positively affect their brands. There's no such thing as "opting out" of these conversations. Your brand is on Twitter, and elsewhere, regardless of whether your company participates or stands idly by.

With Twitter, you'll be able to engage consumers more directly and more intimately than ever before. Twitter is an efficient and cost-effective tool for customer service/support, brand ambassadorship, and marketing. You can use Twitter to converse one-on-one with your customers, improve customer service, reduce costs, and build brand equity.

Transparent Customer Service Has Hidden Benefits

Companies that use Twitter to have public one-on-one conversations with individual consumers are not only providing online customer service but demonstrating their expertise and commitment to customer service in a visible and impactful way.

Twitter's novelty also has PR benefits. Companies that adopt and properly use Twitter now will make big gains with consumers and media for their willingness to be open and transparent in their communications. Zappos, Comcast, and jetBlue, for example, have all received mainstream media praise for their Twitter marketing efforts.

Twitter "Ecosystem" of Supporting Tools and Services

Twitter's extensibility enhances its appeal to communicators. While microblogging may appear to have limited functionality, Twitter, with its highly evolved ecosystem of supporting sites and services, is a powerful communications hub for promoting and distributing content from other social media, including blogs, communities, RSS feeds, and so on. Twitter's API allows third-party developers to create tools that extend Twitter's capabilities and automate connections to other services, broadening Twitter's reach and appeal.

Typical Communications Models

Companies are using Twitter accounts for individual customer service, general customer service, and brand ambassadorship/marketing communications. Many companies use a mixed approach that doesn't fit neatly under any single category. For example, Starbucks uses Twitter for all three of these, to the extent that a coffee company needs to provide individual customer service.

Individual customer service: Comcast is one of the few companies doing live, one-on-one customer service on Twitter. What distinguishes individual customer service is the need to provide consumers with detailed assistance, often technical, in real time. Comcast will "walk" customers through troubleshooting, suggest configurations for hardware and software, and schedule service appointments through their Twitter accounts. The company recently added several accounts to accommodate a growing volume of communications. This strategy is most appealing to IT companies and telecomms (mobile phone, ISP, and cable/broadband). Due to the need for trained personnel, this kind of Twitter account must be staffed with customer support/customer care people who know the company's products and services. It is therefore the most costly use of Twitter. Social network Plaxo is also doing one-to-one customer service on Twitter.

General customer service: Some companies use Twitter to provide general customer service information. Typical updates include airline route and schedule information, service outages, links to customer service sites, store locations, product upgrade announcements, and so on. There is no attempt to provide direct responses to most individual inquiries in real time, although consumers can be referred to the company's website and other resources for assistance. Companies that use this model include Popeyes Chicken and Delta Airlines.

This is a good model for companies who want to improve customer service at a minimal cost. No new content needs to be created, and information comes from existing sources. This is the preferred model for companies with nontechnical products that still need to provide some level of customer service, such as airlines, banks, and retailers. Staffing can be done by the corporate communications or customer service organization.

Brand ambassadorship and marketing communications: This is the most popular model among corporate Twitter users. It is the easiest to staff and update, because it utilizes Twitter as a "managed hub" for the company's existing information outlets like public relations, marketing, corporate social responsibility, and so on. Companies simply post Twitter updates linking to existing content on their websites, blogs, and so on. These updates include new product/service announcements, company financial reports, awards and recognition, events, blog posts and anything else the company wants to promote.

By using Twitter this way, companies will reach a broader audience with company news, and improve brand awareness, but they will miss out on the direct consumer engagement and influence found in the customer service models. Staffing is typically done by the marketing organization. Some companies using this model are Southwest Airlines, Wachovia, and Carnival Cruise Lines, though Wachovia does provide limited customer service as well.

Corporate Communicators Must Understand Twitter's "Permissive" Environment

Twitter's laissez-faire Terms of Service (TOS; the agreement users enter into when they register) requires that corporate communicators apply diligence and a proactive approach. As previously mentioned, services like Twitter can allow "brandjacking," in which people co-opt company names, logos, and so on, and establish bogus, and sometimes malicious, company accounts.

Twitter's TOS is somewhat permissive as it pertains to company names, trademarks, and so on, reserving only "the right to reclaim usernames on behalf of businesses or individuals that hold legal claim or trademark on those usernames." In other words, each company is responsible for its company assets on Twitter and must notify the service of an alleged violation. For this reason, companies must take steps to secure their place on Twitter and other social media sites before trouble arises from unauthorized third-party use.

Establishing a Corporate Presence on Twitter

By following a few simple guidelines, companies can take advantage of Twitter as a customer service and marketing platform:

Tie up your company name now. There is no cost for Twitter registration, which takes just a few minutes at www.twitter/signup. Companies need to sign up even if they don't intend to be active on Twitter, because anyone can take a company's name as a Twitter *handle* and regaining control of the name from another user could involve costly legal action.

Have realistic expectations for Twitter results. You should use Twitter to perform customer service or support; offer promotions for products, services, and events; publish brief updates on company news; and promote the general good of the company through brand "ambassadorship." Dell claims as of June 2008 that it had "surpassed $500,000 in revenue through Twitter, and that number is growing," but it is unusual for most companies to seek direct Twitter revenue. Most value the opportunity for engagement, exposure, and goodwill. Alicia Thompson, VP of communications and PR for Popeyes Chicken, said, "We are still experimenting with social media and have no real expectations. As for results, we have generated a good amount of interest and we are definitely being noticed."

Help consumers validate your presence on Twitter and understand why you are there. Twitter offers little space for companies to display a profile, so make the most of it. Include a description, which can be up to 160 characters in length, as well as a link to your company website. Your Twitter profile must include your company name and the name of the person staffing the account. The background of your Twitter home page and your *avatar* (the icon that represents your company) should be customized to reflect the company logo and brand. Include a link from your company's regular website "news" page to your Twitter profile page.

For example, (**Figure 3.8**) shows the background for the Virgin America Twitter page:

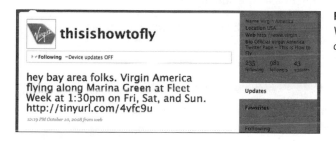

Figure 3.8
Virgin America on Twitter.

Notice the use of the logo, and "this is how to fly" tagline, the link to the company's website, and the identification of this account as "Official Virgin America Twitter Page." The weakness with this example is that Virgin's user ID, thisishowtofly, does not pick up searches on the company's name.

Staff your Twitter account with people who understand the conversational aspect of the medium and have the power to engage on behalf of the company. Staffing strategy for corporate Twitter accounts is highly variable. jetBlue staffs its account with people from its corporate communications organization; Comcast's account is staffed by Frank Eliason, who manages the company's digital care group; and The Home Depot is staffed by a "volunteer" from the company's PR organization who handles Twitter communications in her spare time. Your Twitter representatives must be articulate, well-informed, social media savvy, and empowered to take action on behalf of consumers rather than simply regurgitate company marketing messages. As Twitter's user base grows, and as a company's Twitter account becomes better known, you will probably need to add staff and other resources.

Don't use Twitter in isolation. Link to and from your Twitter account to connect it with other communications initiatives, like a company blog or social media newsroom. Twitter updates are limited to 140 characters but can include links. Shorten links with is.gd, tinyurl.com, and other services, and use them to promote company videos on YouTube, event photos on Flickr, or streaming video via Ustream or Qik, to give Twitter engaging multimedia capabilities.

For a list of companies using Twitter, check out the Fluent Simplicity Twitter Brand Index at http://blog.fluentsimplicity.com/twitter-brand-index/.

Launching an Executive Blog

Most companies should consider launching a blog as part of their social media strategy. A blog can provide a highly efficient and flexible communications vehicle, and it will help the company engage with consumers and others in a much more intimate way than a static website can.

The idea can be daunting, raising questions like:

- Why should we have a blog? (Maybe you shouldn't.)
- Who should blog, how often, on what topics?
- How do we keep our bloggers *on message*, or do we?
- Are there risks to having a blog, and how do we mitigate them?

This book answers many of these questions in a general way, but this section offers some specific considerations for launching a blog and making the most of it.

Although many companies are using internal blogs to allow employees to communicate, and numerous types of external blogs exist, this section deals specifically with external executive blogs; however, many of the same concepts apply to any blogging initiative.

What Is a Blog?

Blogging is the application that triggered the social media revolution. A *blog* is essentially an easily updated website, usually maintained by one or more bloggers (ostensibly, the authors of the content on the blog), identified by name and acting as company spokespeople in the case of a company blog. Built on a Web 2.0 foundation, a blog is easily and quickly updateable by nontechnical professionals, allows easy inclusion of rich media like video and audio, promotes interactive dialogue through comments and other mechanisms, and is highly visible and shareable on the web.

The word is a portmanteau of *web* and *log*, and the earliest blogs were stream-of-consciousness daily activity logs. Like all social media terms, stories as to the origin of the word abound, but the most likely is that the phrase *web log* was first used in 1997 by Jorn Barger, a technology pioneer and early blogger, and was redistributed to *we blog* in 1999 by Peter Merholz.

Technorati, a popular blog search and tagging site, publishes a quarterly "State of the Blogosphere" report on the statistics and demographics of the *blogosphere* (a popular term meaning simply "all the blogs out there.")

According to Technorati's 2008 report, the company has indexed 133 million blogs since 2002 and 7.4 million blog entries were posted in the past 120 days. eMarketer reported in May 2008 that there were 94.1 million U.S. blog readers in 2007 (or 50 percent of Internet users).

Corporate Blogging

As recently as 2007, it was unclear as to whether blogging might become a ubiquitous tool in corporate communications and marketing, but today, more and more companies are coming to understand the powerful communications capabilities of a corporate blog.

The largest, and in some cases most traditional corporations, like Hewlett-Packard, GM, and Southwest Airlines, have blogs. (See the previous section "What's the Buzz Out There?" and "Conversation Monitoring" later for resources useful for finding corporate and CEO blogs.)

Some people think every company's CEO should have a blog, and anyone who doesn't "just doesn't get it." This is absurd. There are many factors affecting the decision to launch a corporate blog. It's not right for every company or every CEO.

Why Blog?

A blog can be a significant part of your marketing and communications effort. Some advantages of a blog are:

- Allows your company's executives to engage in lively interactive conversations with customers, prospects, investors, business partners, media, analysts, and industry peers.

- Positions and differentiates your company's executives as industry leaders who are actively engaged with communities of influence outside the company's four walls.

- Provides a quick, effective mechanism for posting breaking news, announcements, and reactions to news. This is particularly advantageous in crisis communications situations or when reacting to (or breaking) particularly good or bad news about the company.

- Drives traffic to drive to your website, thereby having the potential to generate leads, new business, and increased brand awareness.

- Increases your company's online visibility.

- Enables the use of rich media to improve credibility and drive increased traffic.

- Attracts, creative, high-caliber talent to your company, as they are better exposed to the breadth and depth of your executive team and your company's industry leadership.

A blog is a powerful communications tool and can supplement, or replace, some of the standard corporate communications vehicles. For example, a blog can be used to publish executive viewpoints (statistically the most common use today), quarterly earnings "color commentary," and even the launch of a new product. A blog can be easily updated, so it can be an excellent tool for delivering crisis communications, responding to breaking stories, or simply having the ability to respond to current events in real time.

The idea that the blog can replace some communications tools is important. Budgets are stretched, and executives have a limited amount of time, so balancing blogging with your existing communications mix will be critical to its adoption.

To see how companies are using blogs, check out Constantin Basturea's "New PR Wiki," which has outstanding lists of both CEO blogs and corporate blogs at www.thenewpr.com.

Increasingly, consumers expect the companies they deal with to participate in blogs and other social media. According to *B2B Magazine*, "The '2008 Cone Business in Social Media Study' found that 60 percent of U.S. respondents interact with companies on social media Web sites and that 93 percent believe a company should have a presence in social media."

In addition to the corporate blogs maintained by your competitors, there are probably dozens or even hundreds of influential bloggers writing about your company and your industry. To find out who they are, start with a Google Blog Search on your company name, your industry, your markets, your competitors' names, names of products and technologies, and names of company executives. You can also visit Technorati, click Advanced Search, and do a "Tag Search" on terms similar to the ones mentioned.

With nearly 150 million blogs, there's a good chance that a conversation is going on in the blogosphere about your company and your industry. According to an article in *Online Media Daily*, Coca Cola, for example, reports its brands get "an average of 2,000 blog and 300 Twitter mentions on any given day."

With your own blog, you can join in the conversation, influence it, and advance your company's brand and market perception, or you can sit on the sidelines.

Conversation Monitoring

In addition to Google Blog Search and Technorati, there are numerous methods for monitoring blogosphere conversations to find out what people are saying about your company and your industry. Many of the tools for doing this are discussed in Chapter 7, "Can You Count Everything that Counts?" Here are a couple of suggestions:

- Once you've used Google and Technorati to identify a set of search terms that helps you find appropriate blogs to monitor, establish Google Alerts for these terms, which are email notifications that let you know any time someone publishes something containing these terms. You can elect to receive these reports daily or the moment something is published.

- Use the newsreader in your browser or a dedicated newsreader to have regular updates from important blogs and websites displayed on your desktop. Most web browsers have this capability built in. Google has an excellent newsreader. Bloglines is also a popular newsreader tool.

- Use a "mashup" site like NetVibes (**Figure 3.9**) to aggregate both news feeds and other communications tools. Thanks to RSS feeds and each site or service's API, programmers can easily create applications that combine components from a number of sites to provide users with a more useful single view of their communications activity. NetVibes for example, lets users read as many blogs as they'd like, monitor Facebook and IM, read and respond to email, and perform many other tasks from a single, customized web page. This is often referred to as a *mashup*.

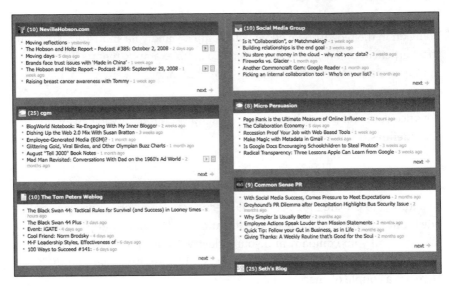

Figure 3.9 *NetVibes home page.*

Using news feeds (also known as RSS feeds) takes some getting used to. Some tools make this transparent to the user, that is, you don't need to know anything about RSS technology. You simply click "subscribe to feed," and the output of a particular blog or website is automatically added to your reader. In other cases, you may need to copy a URL from a blog to a reader. These URLs typically look something like this: http://hungerrelief.tyson.com/rss/rss.ashx.

Objectives: Setting and Measuring

Like any communications initiative, your blog plan should include specific objectives and a strategy for measuring them. Will your blog drive revenue? That might be hard to measure directly, but if your blog is any good, it will drive more traffic to your website, which will in turn drive lead generation and revenue. It will increase brand awareness and improve executive reputation and influence.

Objectives can include things like "improve the company's brand and reputation," and "engage in industry dialogue to promote the company's products and services," but these may also be difficult to measure. More quantifiable objectives, such as "drive 30 percent increase in traffic to website," or "obtain 10,000 downloads for beta software," can also be objectives. Make sure analytics software is in place and functioning correctly prior to launch. (See Chapter 7 for more information on how to measure social media effectiveness.)

Who Should Blog?

Depending on the size of your company and your objectives, any number of people might make good bloggers. In some cases, a company may choose to have just the CEO or a small number of senior executives blog.

Companies with CEO bloggers are very well respected in the blogosphere. Having a CEO blogger positions the company as progressive and genuinely interested in the voice of the marketplace and can contribute to a perception of the CEO as someone who is truly engaged and willing to speak directly to influencers. Although it's impressive to consumers, journalists, and bloggers when a CEO has a blog, not all CEOs have the time, the personality, or the desire to do so.

Beyond the CEO, nearly any other executive at any level in the company is a potential blogger.

Each blogger should support one or more specific aspects of your blogging platform (see the section "The Blogging Platform"). Your "stable" of bloggers could include a visionary, a tech guru, a marketing person, or even a customer support person who together tell a well-rounded story about the company. (And having a group of bloggers divides the workload so that it's easier to keep the blog supplied with fresh content.) What's important is that each blogger has something to say that contributes uniquely to the conversation.

Has anyone in your company written a business or technical book? Is there anyone who has written for a well-known publication and therefore has a "built-in" following that could be leveraged for a blog? Do you have any tech luminaries who are known for industry firsts or innovative thinking? Are there any people in the company who speak regularly at conferences and would have a ready audience? Any of these people is a potential blogger.

The Blogging Platform

The blog should have an overall strategy, such as "engage with vertical market customers 1:1 to communicate our specific value proposition in each of these markets" or "grow the company's credibility and awareness in the financial services industry."

The blogging platform is similar to a speaking platform developed to support executive communications, and identifies themes, topics, key messages, tone, and point of view for the blog and for each blogger.

The choice of appropriate themes and topics for each executive is generally based on the executive's role in the company, but in some cases the executive may have a particularly strong interest and expertise in the topic not necessarily associated with his or her primary role. For example, your chief marketing officer may be particularly knowledgeable and passionate about corporate social responsibility. This person might then be better suited to blog on this topic than on marketing in general.

Your blog must support the company's communications and business objectives, but this does not mean you are creating commercial/marketing-style prose on your blog. One of your biggest challenges will be to create a platform that balances the interests of the company and its shareholders/investors with the desire to create interesting and provocative content that brings readers to the blog.

Your blogging platform will help bloggers stay "on message," but ultimately it is the candid and authentic conversation that takes place on a good blog that draws and retains readers. So, in reality, it is important to let bloggers go a little "off message" sometimes. Too much "marketing speak" and messaging will kill a blog.

Voice, Style, and Content

With the exception of blog posts related to financial/earnings communications bound by SEC and other rules, or those in connection with litigation, posts should be written in a first person, informal style. Although some bloggers pay little or no attention to spelling, grammar, style, and usage, it's important to make a distinction between informal style, which is encouraged, and improper style, which is not.

Corporate bloggers should maintain high standards for spelling, grammar, and usage on their blogs. Personal MySpace-style blogs may include popular web abbreviations, but expressions like "LOL" or "TTFN" are not appropriate in a corporate setting. Remember, your blog is an extension of your website, your corporate identity, and your brand.

Bloggers should write in a conversational tone about things they are genuinely interested in and authoritative about. Blog posts should be relatively short, generally 500 words or less, and need not be formal essays (though sometimes these are useful). Controversy is OK, but it should not be used regularly or insincerely or merely to generate traffic to the blog.

Blog posts need not always be specifically about the company, its products, and so on. In fact, it's very important not to think of the blog as just another marketing vehicle. One CEO blogs about his motorcycle racing experience and relates the lessons he has learned through racing to leadership in the corporate world.

Readers expect that corporate bloggers will:

- Write on relevant, interesting topics.

- Write factually and realistically when talking about the company and its business.

- Not hype the company.

- Not unfairly criticize the competition.

- Provide valuable insights and commentary, not marketing material.

Some bloggers talk about their frustrations with air travel or the hassles of replacing a lost BlackBerry or cell phone. Personal experience can make an interesting "hook" for a blog post, but some of these topics have become trite. The best way to get a sense of proper blog writing style is to read other blogs.

All bloggers should go through some kind of blogger training and sign the company's blogging policy/agreement prior to posting anything. The training should cover blog do's and don'ts, as well as use of the blogging software. (Executives who won't be formatting or publishing their own blog posts won't need to know how to use the software.)

You may want your communications team to review the initial posts drafted by each blogger, but it is not recommended that you do this on a regular basis or that you edit or screen posts in any way. Choose your bloggers well, counsel them, monitor them, and if need be, shut down their blogs if they are not posting in a way that helps you meet your communications objectives. But try not to censor them ahead of time.

Effective Blog Post Writing

Good blog writing is most easily compared to editorial writing. Except for value-based content that might include lists of instructions or an explanation of a technical concept, executive blogging should reflect the executive's personality, experience, and point of view. Posts should be written plainly (unless you are writing for other theoretical particle physicists), in a friendly, conversational tone.

They should not be too conversational however. In the early days of blogging (remember the web log?), trivial posts were commonplace. Although these can strike a chord with readers, they have become trite and largely irrelevant and should be avoided in your blog. The exception would be when such an experience can be used to illustrate a larger concept or to provide a business or leadership "lesson."

Here are a few guidelines:

- Do not harshly criticize competitors. This damages their reputation and yours and can be in violation of FTC and other regulations.

- Do not hype your company and its products too overtly. Be proud of your accomplishments, and those of the company, but keep this to a minimum, and be humble. Too much hype will be seen as marketing spin and readers will stop reading your blog and may criticize it publicly.

- Do not use words you would not use with a customer. Don't use profanity or obscenity. Don't co-opt hipster language unless you are actually hip.

- Avoid industry jargon and unexplained acronyms.

- Do not disclose confidential financial, product, or strategic information.

- Check all your facts carefully. Identify your sources.

- Check spelling, grammar, and usage. You are a public spokesperson of the company.

- If you are referencing another blog post, link back to that post. There are two reasons for doing this. The link provides substantiation and allows the reader to see your original source. Links also improve search engine ranking.

- Insert a relevant image to make your post more lively and engaging, or better still, use video.

Your posts should not be lengthy dissertations. Sometimes a post can be just a few words, like "Check out this fascinating post on the influx of Eastern European start-ups in the Silicon Valley," with a link to the original post.

There are many sources of content ideas for your blog, and there are numerous tools for finding relevant blogs and conversations.

Controversy

In order to be interesting and draw readers and discussion, some bloggers take a controversial or "in-your-face" point of view. This brings with it many risks and potential side effects.

Your bloggers should strive to publish posts that are balanced. It's OK to publish negative or critical posts, but you need to balance these with neutral and positive posts. An all-negative, all-the-time blog is a downer, and this transparent technique will draw many readers initially but will eventually turn off readers.

Another risk associated with excessive controversy is that of alienating a customer or business partner, or drawing one of your competitors into an online feud, which can only harm the reputation of both companies.

Value-Based Content

The very best blog content effectively articulates an opinion consistent with the company's strategy and objectives or offers value-based content that is inherently valuable to customers, journalists, and other people who come to the blog. This category of content generally includes things like "how-to's," case studies, and other content that helps your customers understand the industry landscape and make buying and ROI decisions. Another way to look at value-based content is to think of content that is not product- or company-specific that would be appropriate and interesting even if not posted on the company's blog.

Integration and Implementation Considerations

There are a couple of decisions you have to make based both on your objectives, your IT environment, and your current website architecture and look and feel.

The first of these will be a choice of blogging software. Many blog software platforms are free, and there are dozens available. Some are general-purpose, and others are more suited for an enterprise environment. Some popular blogging environments include:

- WordPress
- Movable Type/TypePad
- Blogger
- Vox

There are many other platforms, but these are a few of the most popular. While every one of these supports all of the popular features of a blog, each may have strengths in a particular area. For example, you'll want to think about the number of bloggers supported by the platform, and whether bloggers will register themselves (create their own accounts on the blog) or whether only an admin (generally the case for a corporate blog) can create new user accounts. Another consideration is graphical customization. Each platform supports some degree of graphics customization (sometimes called *themes*,) but the precise method of customization varies. Your graphic design/web team should evaluate the blogging software you're considering, and weigh in on the kind of capabilities they need.

You will have to work with your corporate IT organization to determine which software will best integrate with the company's current infrastructure, while meeting your requirements for functionality. Most large company IT organizations will want to deploy the blogging environment entirely on their own servers. This is largely based on a desire to own and control the installation, as well as security concerns.

However, many companies are outsourcing entire online communications functions to third parties. For example, a number of large companies use Investor.com to manage their investor communications. In some cases this is evident in the URL for a company's investor relations pages. Whenever you see a URL like *companyname*.investor.com, this may indicate that the page is not hosted internally, but it is hosted elsewhere at what is called a sub-domain. Under this scenario, the investor relations page can be designed to look just like the rest of the regular website so that a visitor to the site is unaware that it is not hosted by the company.

You'll also want to think about the URL for your blog. If you host it on your own servers, you can create a sub-domain, such as blogs.*companyname*.com. Or, you can create a subdirectory, which looks like *companyname*.com/blogs. Finally if your blog is branded with a name that is not the same as your company name, it could be hosted at an entirely independent URL. In any of these situations, there should be a link from the company's main website to the blog, and one on the blog back to the company website.

"Local" Commenting Policy and Moderation

In most cases, your blog should allow comments, meaning visitors to the blog can post comments in response to specific posts. There are exceptions. For example, a blog post reporting on quarterly earnings in compliance with

SEC and Sarbanes-Oxley requirements should not permit comments, as there is potential for inappropriate remarks that might be in violation. If your company is in a highly regulated industry, like pharmaceuticals, you should consult the company's legal department regarding your commenting policy.

Here are a few guidelines regarding comments:

- Comments must *always* be moderated. This means they do not post immediately, but they must be approved by a communications staff member prior to publication.

- Certain comments should never be approved. This includes comments that are inflammatory, obscene, may open the company to legal liability, are totally irrelevant, or simply spam. Your blogging software will capture the IP address of the commenter so that your IT security department can investigate the source of such comment(s) if they wish to do so.

- You should quickly approve ALL comments except those that meet the previous criteria, even if they seem foolish. Many will require judgment calls. For example, there is no reason not to approve "huh?" because it is short hand for "I don't understand this," but you could delete "you're an idiot" because it is inflammatory and not constructive.

- Positive comments, like "love your company," should always be posted quickly. There is no reason to delete these unless you suspect they came from an inappropriate source. Your employees and board of directors should not post anonymous comments, and this should be specifically prohibited by policy. Some companies may choose to disallow all blog comments by people associated with the company, such as employees, suppliers, and board members, even when the commenter is identified, to avoid the appearance of impropriety, but this is very difficult to enforce.

- Negative comments should also be posted quickly, and never edited or deleted. However, you may delay for a short time in order to draft a company response, if one is merited. Think carefully before deleting comments or choosing not to post a particular comment. Companies that have been "caught" in the past deleting comments have been subjected to merciless criticism in the blogosphere. Negative comments are an opportunity to respond on behalf of the company. If someone posts "your support is terrible," this is an opportunity to highlight your world class support organization and defend your company. Be grateful the comment appeared on your site where you can respond and not elsewhere. And if you sent a customer a bad product, or gave them poor support, own up to it, apologize, and let them know the steps you've taken to fix the problem. This will earn the company tremendous respect far in excess of the potential loss of face caused by the original incident. Sometimes, frustrated customers, unable to reach someone in the company who seems to care about their situation, will lash out on a blog, seeing it as their only way to get through to the company.

- Some comments can be controversial and may need to be handled with great care. Any comment that potentially damages or attacks the company, one of its employees or officers, one of its business partners, and so on, in a way that could damage the company's reputation or could put any party in legal jeopardy, needs to be carefully reviewed by the company's communications staff and potentially by company lawyers and finance departments prior to approval/deletion and response.

- Your blogging software should have controls to prevent spam comments. This will save time and reduce the chances of a spam comment being accidentally posted to the blog.

Connections with Other Bloggers

The idea of online conversations is mentioned frequently in this book. An executive blog is one of the principal vehicles for allowing these conversations to take place. As mentioned previously, one conversational element of blogging is commenting, whereby visitors to your company's blog can leave comments, and executives may respond either in the form of additional comments or with an entirely new blog post (when it's called for).

But there are ways to establish a much broader conversation and reach out to other influential bloggers. To do this, you'll need to know how to find these other bloggers (see the section, "Conversation Monitoring") and the process and etiquette for engaging with them online.

Here are three principal ways to engage with external bloggers:

- Leave comments on external blogs.

- Respond to posts on external blogs by publishing a post on your blog.

- Add external blogs to your *blogroll* (list of blogs you read).

When you comment on other blogs, your comment should be relevant, constructive, and brief. Identify yourself clearly as a company representative when commenting on anything remotely related to your role at the company or to the company's business. Keep comments to 125 words maximum, do not criticize overtly, and do not hype your own company or products. If you wish to offer a longer response, post it on your own blog and use the comment to direct people to your response. Use a conversational and respectful tone. Acknowledge the contribution of the original blogger. A typical comment might read:

> "Thanks, Mark, for making some excellent points. I completely agree with your view on outsourcing. I do think those jobs are going to flow back here, though."

You will have the opportunity to provide your name and a link to your blog when you comment. In the outsourcing example, if you had recently written a post on outsourcing, you could add, "I posted on this yesterday," and provide a link to your post. Always use the *permalink* (a permanent link to a particular blog post) when linking to blog posts.

If your intended reply to another blogger's post is going to be much longer than 125 words, you might decide to write a new post as a response instead. Time permitting, this approach has its benefits in that you "own" your blog and have much more latitude (and space) to express your point of view than you would have as a comment on someone else's blog.

Lastly, many bloggers maintain a *blogroll*, which is a list of favorite blogs. The decision to have a blogroll is a matter of preference and depends on the executive's style. If he or she is very informal and engages openly with industry colleagues, a blogroll may be appropriate on a corporate blog. If on the other hand your executive is more formal and reserved, a blogroll may not fit.

If you're unsure how to start one, find a few blogs you like and see who they link to. Bookmark the blogs you like. Once you have a blog, add these to your own blogroll.

Ethical Guidelines and Mitigating Risk

Like nearly all social media, there are risks, both real and perceived, when blogging in a corporate environment. These include risk of:

- Release of sensitive and/or proprietary company information
- Release of financial data prohibited by SEC rules and other financial disclosure regulations
- Unfair competitive statements
- Bloggers "going off message"
- Inappropriate material in comments left by site visitors

It's also important to understand that blogging is just another component of your communications arsenal, and it is not exempt from either the law or common sense. You should remind bloggers that they are still bound by your standards of business conduct and your employee handbook, which caution against unfair competitive practice and guide employee "good faith" behavior as representatives of the company.

Blogger training programs, and specific blogging agreements can help bloggers further understand and avoid these situations. Chapter 6, "Balancing Social Media Risk and Reward," provides extensive guidance on avoiding legal and ethical risk.

Overcoming Personal Fear of Social Media

One of social media's strengths is its ability to allow anyone with a web browser to communicate instantly with potentially millions of people. Whether through a comment on someone else's blog, a new blog of your own, or a comment on a blog or company website, this kind of instant fame, or notoriety, can be a bit scary.

When I coach new bloggers, one thing I encounter frequently is a reluctance to publish their first post. "Is it interesting?" they wonder, "what will people think of it and what will they think of me?" Only somewhat humorously I assure them, "don't worry, no one will read it."

I say this for a couple of reasons. First, unless they make a really serious mistake, statistically, no one *is* going to read their first post. Until a blog, or any other social media effort, has been around a while, and it's been read, commented on, linked to, and referred to, it's still mostly invisible to the world. Secondly, who cares if you say something less than perfect the first time, or the seventeenth time? Another attribute of social media is its ability to bring a personal, human element to communications. If you're old enough to remember, late night television talk show host Johnny Carson was the master of the bombed routine. He was at his best when something went wrong. In the unlikely event your first social media foray results in a gaffe or two, you've got an outstanding opportunity to say, "oops, I made a mistake, I meant to say..." Sounds sort of like a conversation, doesn't it? That kind of honesty and genuineness is a strength, and you will be rewarded for it.

Blogging Terms

blogroll

The blogroll is a list of blogs that you like and read regularly. It appears on the sidebar of your blog. You should add as many relevant and appropriate blogs as possible to the blogroll. Many blog search and ranking tools rank blogs on the basis of authority. A key component of your blog's authority ranking is the number of blogs that link to your blog. When you add a blog to your blogroll, the blog's owner is generally informed that you have done so and may choose to add your blog to his/her blogroll. It is considered bad form, however, to ask others to add you to their blogrolls.

comment

A comment is a response to something someone has posted on his or her blog. Comments are generally much shorter than posts, and there is a specific code of etiquette to posting comments. Readers may post comments on your blog that will be subject to the process and recommendations described earlier. New bloggers should not be disappointed by a low volume of comments. It takes time to build readership, and comments can be few and far between.

news aggregator

A news aggregator is a tool that allows users to subscribe to and display multiple RSS feeds in a convenient format. These can be desktop or web-based applications. Popular news aggregators (aka news readers) are Google Blog Reader (www.google.com/reader), Bloglines (www.bloglines.com), and NetVibes (www.netvibes.com). News aggregators are described in more detail elsewhere in the book.

permalink

The primary link to your blog might be something like http://blogs.company.com/. The permalink, on the other hand, is a permanent link to a particular blog post, and might look like http://blogs.company.com/09-09-innovation/. Many people make the mistake of directing others to their main blog URL when they meant to direct them to a particular post. You should always use the permalink for this purpose. It can usually be seen by clicking the title of the post, or there may be a link marked "permalink" somewhere on the post.

continues on next page

Blogging Terms *(continued)*

ping

The term *ping* is borrowed from networking, but it means something slightly different in the world of blogs. A ping occurs when you publish a blog post, and your blogging software notifies external websites that your blog has been updated. These in turn notify other sites and services so that your new content is propagated to multiple destinations, such as blog search engines, across the web. Your blog should at the very least ping Google and Technorati. There are also services such as Pingomatic, which ping multiple sites. Do not attempt to ping too often, as this may result in your blog being banned from some search engines and sites.

post

The text that you publish on your blog is called a post. These are generally identified by date, time, and sometimes topic.

RSS feed

RSS stands for really simple syndication. Your blog is equipped with an RSS feed that allows users to subscribe to receive regular updates from your blog. Whenever your blog is updated, your RSS feed is updated as well. It will generally function in a way that is invisible to you.

tags and keywords

Tags and keywords should be attached to every blog (this is done at the implementation level) and to every blog post (which is done during editing and is the responsibility of the blogger.) Keywords and meta tags are the terms that regular search engines, such as Google and Yahoo, use to find a page. Those at the top level—for example, those embedded in the blog home page—should refer to the blog and the company in general terms.

Tags and keywords associated with the post should be specific to that post, and the words or phrases used should be repeated one or more times in the body of the post. In addition to regular HTML tags, you should add Technorati tags with every post. For more information on Technorati tags, see http://support.technorati.com/faq/topic/47?replies=1.

trackback

A trackback is similar to a comment, except it is automatically generated. A trackback occurs whenever someone links to your blog from his or her blog. A trackback is similar in appearance to a comment, but it is usually bracketed with [...].

It's OK to ask for help. Social media is all about taking advantage of the wisdom of the many. No matter what its size or industry, there are undoubtedly people in your organization who can be extremely useful resources in developing your social media strategy. These people are often referred to as social media evangelists or digital champions. They are typically, but not always, younger people who grew up digital, spent years on MySpace and Facebook before corporate communicators ever heard of social networks, and are extremely comfortable adapting to and using Web 2.0 tools as they become available. They also understand the etiquette of social media—but a word of caution here, there is a big difference between appropriate etiquette for personal use of social media and the right way to use corporate social media.

These digital champions can help you understand the landscape of existing tools and can be critical in evangelizing your social media programs inside the company. I have not yet found an avid social media user who is not anxious to share knowledge with others.

So far the discussions have included the benefits of social media in a corporate communications environment, including immediacy, authenticity, and improved engagement with customers and other influencers. The next chapter will talk about how your social media strategy can take advantage of these attributes, how you can select and configure the appropriate tools, and how you can balance this new level of open participatory communications with the need to maintain a certain amount of control over your brand and your message.

Now What?

Now that you're familiar with most of the basic social media tools that you might apply in corporate communications, you're probably asking yourself, now what?

As mentioned in Chapter 1, "Social Media Goes Corporate," your social media strategy and business objectives will drive your selection of the appropriate social media tools. In Chapter 4, "Can You Control Your Brand, or Just Share It?," we'll spend a little more time explaining how to develop that social media strategy.

In the meantime, if you are not already using these tools, the best approach is to jump in now. If you're not already reading some blogs, go find some interesting ones, build a blogroll, and think about what it is about the blogs you do read that makes them appealing. If you want to create your own blog or manage a blog for your company, this experience will be invaluable.

Get on LinkedIn and network with professional contacts. Sign up for Twitter and try it out for a couple of weeks. (You won't get any value out of it until you put some time in it, and once you do you'll be shocked that you've lived without it.)

If you want to make social media a part of your work life, find out what your company is doing and what others in the industry are doing, and then volunteer to help or start something new.

Can You Control Your Brand, or Just Share It?

Perceptions about "control" of the brand have caused some companies hesitation when it comes to adopting social media. They fear that giving too much control to outsiders will adversely affect the company's brand. In a world of consolidation and globalization, where the physical product is only a part of the company's differentiation, brand attributes have become increasingly important. Earlier, I mentioned that the CEO of Procter & Gamble suggested companies "let go" of their brands, yet this suggestion came from the chief executive of a company that created the position of brand manager. Clearly there is conflict here.

But these concerns come from both a misunderstanding of just what a brand is, and notions of whether a company actually *can* control its brand.

A company's brand is not merely its logo and company name. It's something far greater. Some companies, like Disney and Coca-Cola, do exert very strong control over certain elements of their brands, such as trademarks, images, logos, and product names. Many companies have made major investments in these components and are rightly concerned about managing them to best advantage.

Any discussion of social media implications to the corporate brand must begin with a definition of brand, and some agreement as to just whether the company can control its brand, manage it, share it, or must give it over to the whims of consumers.

Merriam Webster defines brand as

> "a class of goods identified by name as the product of a single firm or manufacturer."

True, but not very useful for this discussion.

David Ogilvy, often called the *father of advertising*, defined a brand as

> "the intangible sum of a product's attributes: its name, packaging, and price, its history, its reputation, and the way it's advertised."

I define a brand as the sum total of our experiences with a company, its products, services, and employees, and the way those experiences shape our perception of the company.

Under these broader, modern definitions, it becomes obvious that a company cannot own or control its brand. It can, however, manage its brand, and, thanks to social media, participate more actively in discussions that affect its brand.

It's unlikely that at any time in history companies were truly able to control their brands. However, with each successive generation of communications tools, the idea that a company owns its brand exclusively has grown increasingly harder to support. Perhaps one hundred years ago, when electronic communications was in its infancy, there were only a few channels through which the voice of consumers could be heard and amplified. Over the course of media history, various developments, such as broadcast news, and later on, the web, gave new voice to consumers.

With the advent of social media, consumer voices have grown exponentially louder, and online conversations have begun more and more to shape a company's brand. Smart companies recognize this fact, and as part of their social media strategy, embrace it and take advantage of it.

So just how much "control" is possible in the world of social media, and how much is desirable? And when is it advantageous for a company to loosen its perceived grip on the brand?

Corporate Identity in Social Media

One issue that will come up for nearly every large company is the ownership, use, and misuse, of the company's corporate identity. This includes the company's name, logo, website URLs, product names, and other visual elements associated with the company's brand.

Not only will the company want to properly employ its identity in its own social media initiatives, but there will be circumstances under which the company will need to review unauthorized third-party use of its identity and make decisions on what, if anything, to do about it. In some cases it may actually be desirable for the company to "look the other way" when third parties use the company's name without the company's approval.

Let's begin with some suggestions for securing elements of the company's brand, and then look at situations in which, instead of policing the brand, the company might be better off "sharing" it with consumers.

"Managing" the Company's Message

Messaging is an important part of your communications strategy and is therefore important to your social media strategy. As I've mentioned elsewhere in the book, social media are merely a new set of communications tools, which will require learning and understanding, but to which the following common sense, and tried and true communications practices still apply:

- Messaging is still important. There are key ideas you would like to convey about your company, whether through traditional channels or through social media, like blogs.

- There are ways to stay on message authentically. Don't edit executive social media content like blog posts. Loosely tie social media initiatives to marketing messages but don't parrot marketing buzzwords or taglines.

- Communications must be two-way. The corporation must participate in the conversation.

- Communications alone can't fix most things. True participatory communications and multi-dimensional discussion mean not only does the company give people a means of discussion, but that the company listens and responds to what's being said, and it empowers all of its people to do so as well.

- Negative buzz about your company is not something to be squelched but rather an opportunity to regain control of the agenda.

- With common sense, knowledge of what works and what doesn't, and understanding of social media etiquette, training, and policies, nearly any company can engage in low-risk, high-value social media. These are the keys to managing your social media programs in a way that will build your brand and will actively involve customers and others in the process.

Many large companies have specialists or entire groups devoted to messaging. In order to achieve the company's business objectives, it is desirable to identify the specific audiences the company wishes to reach and the messages most appropriate for each audience.

Audience

The word *audience* is fraught with emotion for many, and some social media purists have even called for the elimination of the word itself, because it suggests one-way communications to a captive and silent group. For the purposes of this book, audience is used in a corporate communications context. Every communications effort requires the identification of influencers—analysts, shareholders, employees, journalists, and so on—that can be referred to as audiences, and it requires some thought as to the key messages that need to be conveyed to each of these audiences. It would be impossible to develop messages or determine who to communicate them to without some concept of audience.

There are many ways to ensure that the company's messages are incorporated into your social media programs without compromising authenticity, credibility, and spontaneity. As in any other form of corporate communications, it's wise to guide the participants in your social media programs to help them best support your overall communications strategy by providing them with messaging documents, editorial calendars/guidelines, briefings, and other tools that you normally use for this purpose.

In terms of messaging, there are several major distinctions between social media and traditional communications channels. The processes that underlie your social media programs must be very subtle and must not interfere with authenticity, conversational tone, immediacy, and other characteristics that make social media so effective. The "output" of your social media programs will be subject to fewer internal reviews, and in some cases to no review whatsoever.

An executive blog is one example of a social media program in which it is not that difficult to introduce some degree of messaging and thematic oversight. Many communicators are worried that the CEO and other executives will not be able to stay on topic, or they will wander far from the discussions that are important to the company's business goals. This is a situation requiring careful consideration. Many would argue that any degree of influence over an executive blogger would result in a lack of authenticity or credibility, or worse, introduce too much marketing hype into the equation. You must remember, however, that all your communications vehicles belong to the company and have a job to do. They can all be maintained in a way that retains the virtues of authenticity, credibility, transparency, and so on, while still allowing you to use them to achieve business and communications results.

Although it is not acceptable for marketing to write the CEO's blog posts, for example, it is both acceptable and smart for the CEO's communications team to provide some kind of input as to the topics, themes, and points of view they want the CEO to project.

One way to communicate these key messages or themes to any of the company's bloggers is to provide regular briefings on appropriate topics. A more formal approach is to use an *editorial calendar* that outlines well in advance key events and milestones and the timing and themes for blog posts in support of these.

Another element of your blogging program should be blogging platforms. These are short documents identifying a handful of key themes that each blogger should focus on and key messages that the blogger needs to convey. I always suggest a balance when guiding bloggers on what to write about. You should design messaging documents and platforms that guide the writing, but provide enough latitude to allow the blogger to write on any relevant and interesting topic.

The art of balancing the company's strategic communications objectives with spontaneous, engaging writing is what defines a good company blog. It is only through experience, a pragmatic approach, and constant course correction that your company's blog and other social media initiatives will achieve this balance.

Locking Up Your Company's Social Network Identity

Social media, with its often loose standards regarding user identity, has opened up a Pandora's Box of opportunities for confusion about who is, and isn't, an authorized company spokesperson.

One step you can take to secure certain elements of your brand, and to avoid such confusion, is to register the company's name on as many popular social networks and social media sites, like Twitter, MySpace, and Facebook, as possible. Unfortunately, nearly without exception, these sites will allow anyone to register any company name without authentication. The user agreements for these sites, sometimes called the Terms of Service (TOS), often leave it to the owners of company names and brand names to police the names online.

Brandjacking

Lack of controls on many social media sites has resulted in numerous instances of *brandjacking*, the unauthorized use of a company's brand. Some of these are good humored, others can cause problems for companies, and many are actually quite positive and beneficial.

Although I previously made recommendations for controlling the company's brand identity online ahead of time, there are often situations in which corporate communicators, sometimes urged on by the company's legal department when trademark and copyright violations occur, must make judgments regarding unauthorized use as it comes to the company's attention. These decisions should be made on the basis of the benefits versus the potential harm to the company presented by each case. It is not always to the company's benefit to crack down on every unauthorized use of its logo, product photography, name, and so on.

This is a difficult concept for many companies to understand, after many years of very strict regulation of these things. Marketing 101 tells us that we should not allow unauthorized use of the company's name, logo, and product photos. However, this is not Marketing 101—it's social media. Smart companies need to recognize that the rules have changed.

There are many occasions when a company's brand is brandjacked for the better. A search on nearly any popular company or product on Facebook will reveal dozens of Facebook groups and pages devoted to the company, most of them not authorized by the company. For example, a search on Facebook groups for *Bang and Olufsen* reveals over 50 groups devoted to the company and its products. Many of these feature the company's logo, official product photography, and links to the company's website. It is difficult to tell which are authorized by the company, and ironically, several claim to be "the only official Bang and Olufsen Facebook page." There are thousands of groups like these on Facebook, often using copyright logos and images.

There are over 500 Facebook groups devoted to Apple products, nearly all of which are not approved by the company. Note that together, the four shown in **Figure 4.1** account for over 45,000 Apple enthusiasts (though there may be some overlap) and all are showing recent growth in membership.

Figure 4.1 *Facebook groups devoted to Apple products.*

Unauthorized Social Media Use: Shut It Down or Let It Be?

If you're in marketing communications, charged with policing the company's identity, you need to look at each situation of unauthorized brand use and ask yourself what are the benefits associated with letting the public do as they please with your corporate identity and your brand versus the benefits of shutting down an unauthorized use. Some companies, wisely, choose to look the other way. If the results are positive, why not let consumers do your marketing?

A quick scan through the discussions going on in these unauthorized Facebook pages, and those on other networks, reveals that the participants are often quite favorable toward a company. If you can get hundreds or even thousands of people posting positive remarks about your company, it can be quite beneficial, and in that case you might want to leave well enough alone.

Even if the comments are negative, they serve as an invaluable source of customer satisfaction information, and they might provide an opportunity for the company to weigh in and correct misconceptions. No difficult situation was ever made better by prohibiting its discussion.

If on the other hand discussions on a particular page or within a particular group are highly negative, you might want to consider taking steps to either close it down, or perhaps more effectively, to join in the conversation and take advantage of the opportunity to improve your company's brand through positive consumer engagement. One approach is to have an official company representative join the group, and participate actively in the discussion. To do so, you would have to identify yourself as a company spokesperson, act in good faith on behalf of the company, have the knowledge necessary to respond to questions, and have the power to do something in response to what you learn through your interactions.

You could choose to close down the unauthorized use by contacting the owners of the social network or site and requesting that they do so. In some cases, legal action may be required, bringing with it potential for backlash.

This was the case with a widely publicized example of brandjacking involving Scrabulous, a Facebook version of the popular Hasbro word game Scrabble. Scrabulous.com was launched by two brothers, Jayant and Rajat Agarwalla, in 2006, and the Facebook application was launched in June, 2007. The game soon had over 2 million users, and tens of millions of daily page views. Claiming infringement, Hasbro and Mattel forced Facebook and the brothers to pull the game.

This raises some questions. First of all, for the corporate communicator charged with "policing" the brand, this situation might have presented an opportunity and not a problem. With millions of users, could Mattel and Hasbro have leveraged Scrabulous to promote the retail board game? And as an online version of the game, which could be played out over weeks and months between strangers on different sides of the planet, was Scrabulous really eating into sales of Scrabble? Apparently, the game makers were also in talks with electronic game maker Electronic Arts to produce an online version of Scrabble, so Scrabulous may have interfered with that. So why not buy Scrabulous?

However, Hasbro and Mattel did eventually determine that the potential of Scrabulous to erode its brand, and its revenue, was greater than any benefit achieved by allowing it to continue to exist, and prevailed on Facebook to remove the game. An unfortunate outcome of this decision was that it made more than 2 million Scrabulous users very unhappy with the company.

Identifying Company Spokespeople

In the social media world, companies are being required to do something they've never done before—they are being called upon to establish their corporate identity in a third-party environment over which they have little or no control.

An emerging area of concern is the appropriate identification of company spokespeople. In order for an environment of trust to be created online, consumers need to know to whom they are talking. On some networks, anyone can create an account using a company name without having to show authorization to use that name.

Often the Terms of Service (conditions for participation in a particular social network or site) are loosely written and loosely enforced, leaving plenty of room for abuse by both malicious and mischievous individuals falsely posing as company representatives. It's also popular to impersonate celebrities and politicians on Twitter. In the run-up to the 2008 election, there were several people on Twitter representing themselves as Republican vice-presidential candidate, Sarah Palin, though none of them were genuine.

In the corporate world, there are often unauthorized uses of a company's name and identity that are not necessarily damaging but might be cause for concern. In 2008, for example, ExxonMobil confirmed that "Janet," who staffed an account on Twitter called ExxonMobilCorp, was not an authorized representative of the company. "Janet" was a hard fraud to spot. She was using the company name and logo, and her Twitter profile used ExxonMobil branding to round out the illusion. She was also knowledgeable about the company and the energy industry in general.

The revelation that Janet had perpetrated a hoax spurred a flurry of reactions, including observations that social media is inherently untrustworthy, and that companies, like Twitter, that run these networks, don't do enough to police the use of company and personal identities. Arguably, a company like ExxonMobil, in a demanding regulatory environment and a frequent target of attacks by environmentalists, probably needs to maintain closer control of spokespeople, company authorized and otherwise.

It's unclear whether ExxonMobil took steps to shut down the account. Biz Stone, Twitter co-founder, contacted via email, would not comment on whether ExxonMobil had asked them to reclaim the user name, saying only

"Twitter responds to requests from company representatives with a policy that supports trademark, brands, and businesses. If there is a conflict with our Terms of Service, companies can contact us and we'll work to get it resolved."

Twitter's Terms of Service does not specifically ban misrepresentation as an authorized company representative, and it states,

"We reserve the right to reclaim user names on behalf of businesses or individuals that hold legal claim or trademark on those user names."

In other words, if a company specifically requests it, Twitter may take back a user name. In the meantime, there are many issues to be settled in regards to corporate identity outside the four walls of the corporation.

Establishing Corporate Identity in Social Media

For corporations with a legitimate presence on social networks, full disclosure is mandatory. Companies like JetBlue, Zappos, Popeyes Chicken, Dell, and GM have done an outstanding job of this. On Twitter, for example, Dell employees generally append *Dell* to their online identities, using names like RichardAtDell to make it clear they represent the company.

For consumers, there are several ways to verify the authenticity of a social network identity, and companies should do everything possible to help them make these determinations. Each network has a user profile that should include a link to a company website, and should employ some form of brand identity. Until business use of social networks is more established, companies need to take steps to assure consumers they are talking to an authorized company representative. To provide additional validation, you should add your company's social network affiliations to the corporate news page on your website. This will also create awareness and drive traffic to your social network activities.

One company that has done a nice job of identifying its social network affiliation on its corporate website is Wachovia. They have placed a simple banner that promotes and links to their Twitter account (**Figure 4.2**). In the small space of a banner ad, perhaps the only place on the web other than Twitter where space is so limited, Wachovia has not only validated its presence on Twitter but has explained that a consumer could subscribe to "get updates via Web or cell phone."

In time, social networks may introduce and enforce more restrictive Terms of Service to protect consumers and corporations alike and to make the services

more valuable as corporate communications tools. Without an assurance of trustworthiness, all forms of social media are useless to bona fide businesses.

Figure 4.2 *Wachovia provides links to their Twitter account.*

Guidelines for Managing Your Social Media Corporate Identity

Your company needs to take positive steps to manage your corporate identity. The following four rules have already been discussed, but they deserve repeating. They are intended to guide the legitimate company in protecting its identity, building trust with consumers, and assuring them that they are dealing with an authorized company representative empowered to speak on behalf of the company and to help them if they have a problem:

o **Create an online profile that helps people verify your affiliations.** Dozens of purported companies (and celebrities) on social networks have turned out to be bogus. Link your online profile to your company website to give consumers a place to go if they have questions. Use your company logo as your *avatar* (profile picture) and use it in supporting graphics. For fun, you can subscribe to Chuck Norris's updates on Twitter, but know that you aren't actually "hearing" from the real Chuck Norris.

o **Let consumers know who they are talking to.** Explain briefly who is staffing your page or account. For example: "This page is managed by John Stevens of our customer support organization."

o **Publish your social media affiliations on your website.** List your company's social media affiliations on the news page of the company website. This allows consumers, journalists, and bloggers to quickly verify which social media identities are authorized by the company.

o **Live and let live.** Weigh the risks and benefits of any unauthorized use of your corporate identity before reacting. Often, there are hidden benefits that outweigh traditional concerns about logos, trademarks, and so on.

U-Haul—A Missed Customer Service Opportunity

You've probably heard it said that there is a conversation going on out there and that your company needs to participate. But what does that really mean? It means that across a universe of millions of blogs, online communities, social networks, and so on, day in and day out, people are publishing comments about your company—some good, and some not so good. Potentially, thousands and even millions of people can also read these comments. And because they are published using Web 2.0 technology, they are widely disseminated via RSS feeds, Google alerts, search, and other methods.

These discussions can be extremely valuable to a company that knows how to respond to them. First of all, they serve as a rich source of general customer satisfaction data. Although it is mostly anecdotal, it can be quite useful and enlightening. Oftentimes, you'll find company *boosters*—people who evangelize the company.

By "listening" to online conversations, a company can become aware of a particularly acute customer satisfaction issue, like the one faced by truck rental company, U-Haul, in apparent blissful ignorance. David Alston, a Twitter user, and someone familiar with the power of social media, complained online about an experience he had with the company. Others joined in, most of them echoing David's sentiment that U-Haul had provided poor customer service. This was more than just a rant session. This was a deliberate grassroots effort to get the company's attention by complaining in a public forum. Here are a few of the comments:

o "Horrendous service...fails on many levels...poorly maintained trucks, too."

o "I'm going to need a moving truck soon...maybe I should try another company this time around"

o "Abysmal customer service"

o "I have had way too many problems with them — bad equipment, oversold equipment, and so on."

A company with even the most superficial presence on Twitter could have managed this situation, but instead it snowballed as angry consumers added their experiences and company spokespeople slept soundly at their desks. U-Haul did not offer any public response.

As Alston summarized it

> "Here we have a well-known North American brand seemingly oblivious to the goings-on in social media and to the pent-up frustration with its brand."

So where were the company's representatives and spokespeople while all this was going on? Wherever they might have been, they were completely ignorant of this groundswell of consumer discontent. And once apprised of it, they simply chose to ignore it.

It would be naive to say a company "has" to be on Twitter, but with the low cost of entry and the opportunity to get involved in and learn from some of these discussions (and possibly head some of them off before they become blog posts and social media failure case studies), why wouldn't you? And you don't need to have a Twitter account to monitor these conversations. Here are a few ways to monitor the chatter:

o Create a Google news and blog alert using your company's name as the search term, and have a daily or immediate email sent to you every time something is published online mentioning your company.

o Make a habit of searching your company name on Technorati, Google, and Twitter search (search.twitter.com).

o Sign up on Get Satisfaction (getsatisfaction.com) to participate in consumer discussions about your company.

o And of course more importantly, be prepared to respond to these situations. In a difficult situation, offer the customer a remedy and be very open about your willingness to "make things right."

Alston eventually exchanged emails and voicemails with the CEO of U-Haul, but he ultimately rented with another company. Maybe U-Haul sees this as anecdotal customer discontent that doesn't merit attention through its regular customer service channels, but there are at least 100 people who have openly said they are unhappy with the company's service and got no response. That seems like a missed opportunity.

Using Social Media to Reach the Right People

Advertising is as old as free enterprise itself. Public relations was *invented* by Edward Bernays and/or Ivy Lee in the early 20th century, and formal use of the concept of marketing came along in the 1960s. All of these forms of specialized communications came out of the recognition by businesses and politicians that success was dependent on communicating with certain groups of people.

Dozens of specialized communications functions exist within any large company, whether within corporate communications, marketing, or some other organization, and nearly every one of these functions is adopting social media.

The degree to which each communications function within a company embraces social media varies greatly. The most common social media initiatives are designed to reach journalists (media), customers, and, increasingly, bloggers. Meanwhile, it's no secret that internal and employee communications are not typically the first to adopt new communications technology. This is not specific to social media and generally reflects a company's business objectives and prioritization of its most important audiences and its resources.

Yet nearly everyone who might be reached by corporate communications con-tributes to the success or failure of the business, and a good social media strategy involves customers, journalists, shareholders, investors, analysts, employees, business partners, and dozens of other important groups of people. Your customers buy products, generating revenue and paying the bills. Your employees power business operations and in some cases serve as the "voice" of the company with customers. Journalists and analysts help consumers and businesses make purchasing and investment decisions. Chapter 3, "What Are Social Media and Web 2.0?," covered a wide range of social media tools used in corporate communications, but the intent of this chapter is to provide some examples of audience-specific social media programs.

Finally, keep in mind as you read these examples that in the new media world, there are all kinds of conversations going on out there that you need to participate in, or possibly initiate. Perhaps one of the most profound changes brought on by social media is that reaching the right people means being prepared to engage in conversations where people "live" on the web: Facebook, MySpace, Twitter, LinkedIn, specialized customer support forums, and anywhere else people are being influenced not only by companies but by their friends and associates.

Employee Engagement

Increasingly, companies are looking beyond external audiences and recog-nizing the importance of employees in their social media strategy. In some cases, social media is used internally to improve collaboration and commu-nications within the employee community, and in other cases companies are giving employees the freedom to serve as "ambassadors" on external social networks like Twitter and Facebook. In addition to the following examples, please see Chapter 8, "SocialCorp 2.0: Corporate Communications Inside Out," for more examples of innovative ways companies are using social media to engage with employees.

Zappos

Online shoe retailer Zappos encourages its workforce to use the microblog-ging tool Twitter. More than 200 Zappos employees send updates to Twitter during the course of their workday. Zappos highlights the initiative by aggre-gating all of its employees' tweets onto a special page on their corporate website: http://twitter.zappos.com/employee_tweets.

To motivate employees to use Twitter, Zappos encouraged competition between employees by using a leader board to track the number of Twitter followers each employee gained. Zappos, like many companies venturing into social media for the first time, had initial concerns regarding the potential for employees to post inappropriate content, but this has not turned out to be a problem.

Zappos CEO, Tony Hsieh, plays a very active role on Twitter. In a tutorial on their website, Hsieh explains the value of the service to skeptics:

> "Remember back when sending SMS text messages on your cell phone was a new thing, and it seemed kind of strange to use your cell phone to do that? And today, you probably wonder how you ever lived without text messaging.

> Well, Twitter is the same way. It's going to seem a little weird at first, but I promise you if you can talk your friends into joining it and you all use it for two weeks, it will change your life. You will wonder how you ever lived without it."

Zappos is an ideal case study in how to help employees understand and embrace the benefits of social media. First, a senior executive endorsed the initiative and took a very visible lead role. Tony Hsieh demonstrated the utility of the service by using it daily and evangelizing its value. Second, the company encouraged employee involvement through friendly competition and by dedicating company IT resources to the implementation. Finally, by giving employees the freedom to use Twitter, Zappos demonstrated that the company was serious about transparency and that it had confidence in the good judgment of its employees.

Zappos also uses Twitter to facilitate informal strategic partnerships. Zappos creates Twitter tracking pages for highly influential fans of their products, such as the Zappos Twitter page for popular wine and social media expert Gary Vee: http://twitter.zappos.com/garyvee.

The initiative has paid off for the online retailer. In addition to *tweeting* about their work lives, employees tastefully and subtly recommend company products and promotions to their followers. They also use Twitter to help resolve customer support issues.

IBM

IBM is experimenting with a variety of social networks for employees. According to a May 22, 2008 report in *Business Week*, these include Dogear, a community-tagging system based on Delicious; and Blue Twit, an enterprise version of Twitter. Dogear is a social bookmarking service that is used to store and share links of interest. IBM employees use Dogear as a knowledge storage and management tool that enables them to share news and articles of interest. Blue Twit is used among employees to communicate and track internal conversations.

Beehive, an IBM internal social network, has 30,000 users. *Business Week* reports Beehive has a popular feature called the Top Five list:

> "People can make lists of their Top Five anything, such as the five projects they're proudest of, five technologies they can't live without, or the five best meals they've had in Paris. People come up with new lists, and others follow. Like much of social media, it mixes the personal with the professional—and each person has to figure out for him- or herself where to draw the line."

Employees use Beehive as a way to share ideas and interact with colleagues around the world. IBM is home to 400,000 employees working in cross-functional global teams. Many lack the luxury of stopping by a colleague's cubicle to catch up, and instead they rely on social tools like Beehive that facilitate these interactions in an online setting.

Devoting company resources to the development of enterprise social networks and gaining senior-level participation were essential to IBM's successes.

Intel

Larry Shoop, Director of Employee Communications at Intel, says the company makes broad use of social media for internal communications. Shoop said,

> "Social media allows a sharing of common skills, expertise, experience, and interests that strengthens the shared knowledge of the organization, offers efficiency gains through collaboration, and brings people together both professionally and personally in meaningful ways."

According to Shoop, Intelpedia is one of the primary social media applications that has really taken off and succeeded at Intel. Intelpedia has gone from dozens of entries just a couple of years ago to over 10,000 entries today.

It is a rich repository of relevant, important, accurate information regarding key Intel products, technologies, and strategies.

Figure 5.1 *The main page of Intelpedia.*

Shoop says more companies are realizing that social media is second nature to younger employees who see it as a highly credible source of information. In addition to Intelpedia, Intel has numerous internal executive blogs, including one done by the CEO. According to Shoop, the CEO doesn't post quite as often as he'd like, but when he does, the blog is

> "read by 50 percent to 75 percent of the employee population. Plus, he keeps the posts opinionated and clearly offers perspectives that can only come from a CEO, whether it's a (report on a) meeting with the president on Intel's charitable and volunteer activities or some inside information on a key business deal or decision. Plus, he frequently responds personally to employees who make comments to his blog."

Analyst and Investor Relations

Industry analysts, financial analysts, and shareholders play an extremely important role in the company's success and should also be included in a companywide social media strategy. Many efforts originating in public relations will also be effective in reaching industry analysts, but there is also the potential for analyst-specific social media initiatives. Companies are also beginning to use social media tools to reach financial analysts and shareholders.

Communications to these people are generally the responsibility of analyst relations (AR) and investor relations (IR) groups in larger corporations. More than most, their communications are bounded by strict regulation. Analyst-specific social media is still in its infancy, but it shows promise.

Cisco has launched a series of analyst relations blogs at blogs.cisco.com/ar to cater to several of their analyst audiences. Cisco has used the blog to share their intent to acquire Jabber, Inc. and to announce feature enhancements to a video product, for example.

Dell IR uses Twitter to keep analysts and investors informed of breaking news at www.twitter.com/dellshares. Dell also maintains DellShares, an IR-specific blog at http://dellshares.dell.com.

The IR Web Report (www.irwebreport.com/) is a good source for information on what companies are doing in online IR.

PR agency Hill & Knowlton launched an analyst relations blog in September 2006 as a "forum for mutual learning about all things AR," promising to "share lessons learned from fantastic mistakes." The blog features a list of over 70 analyst blogs.

In December 2007, Carter Lusher and Dave Eckert, both formerly of Hewlett-Packard AR, launched SageCircle, an online community designed to help companies learn how to work with analysts and use their research.

Blogger Relations

Having come to understand the unique role played by influential bloggers, many companies are establishing specialized blogger relations functions that fill a role similar to that of traditional media relations. Just as each traditional journalist has his or her own beat, editorial strategy, and preferred method for being "pitched," so too do bloggers who are in their own way simply online journalists.

Like everything in social media, pitching bloggers has its etiquette and its potential pitfalls. A number of high-profile bloggers have become extremely vocal about what they perceive as inappropriate pitching by PR professionals, going so far as to publish the email addresses of their "black lists" of people from whom they will not accept a pitch.

That does not, however, excuse the profession from being smart about working with influential bloggers. Here are some brief suggestions for doing this:

- **When pitching bloggers, there is no correct way for all bloggers.** There is a correct way for each blogger. Some online research will tell you whether the blogger prefers email, a Facebook message, a phone call, or some other method.

- **Get to know the blogger before making the pitch.** Read his or her blog thoroughly and often, comment on the blog, link to the blog, go to the same industry events, look at the companies, industries, and themes the blogger covers, and how. Take the blogger out for drinks. Do the homework.

- **It's called media relations, or blogger relations, for a reason.** It works only when there are trusted relationships. Don't pretend to have a relationship with someone when you don't. You need to actually have one, and maintain it, and apply the rules of relationships. Be honest, respond on a timely basis, give the other person communications with value, don't manipulate, or if you must manipulate, admit to it.

Don't think your Facebook messages, Twitter direct messages, emails, or any other seemingly privileged correspondence is off-limits. Apply the old rule "don't put anything in writing in any form unless you don't mind seeing it on the front page of *The New York Times*." Or a widely read blog.

Customer Service, Support, and Engagement

Social media offers companies an opportunity to provide more personalized customer service and support, and in many cases to reach consumers where they spend their time (a social network or Twitter, for example), rather than requiring them to visit a separate site every time they need help from a company they do business with. Some companies, like Comcast and Plaxo, are using Twitter for one-on-one customer support, providing specific technical guidance and troubleshooting, live, online, with consumers. Others do online customer service in a more generalized way, using social networks and other tools to refer customers to appropriate resources.

No social media program, no matter how effective, can take the place of a quality product or good customer service, but many companies are finding that social media is an extremely effective way of improving customer service. Due to the highly visible, public nature of these interactions, many companies are also experiencing improved reputations.

Dell

Some would say that Dell learned its social media lessons the hard way. In June 2005, a blogger coined the Internet meme "Dell Hell" by tearing into Dell's poor customer service. The blogger implored Dell to start participating in online social forums and to join the conversation customers were having about the company.

On the heels of the controversy, Dell started to leverage a wide variety of social media platforms for customer engagement. They went a step further and became active participants in online spaces. The most notable example is Direct2Dell, a company blog about Dell products, services, and customers. Many posts reveal a sense of humility and interest in customer feedback including the open confession, "we blew it." This was a good first step in defusing negative discussions about the brand online.

Both executives and employees post to the blog, answering questions and facilitating customer support issues. With 30 to 50 or more posts a month, Dell is actively engaging with its global customer base, and there are Chinese, Spanish, Norwegian, and Japanese versions of the Direct2Dell blog.

In addition to blogging in different languages, Dell hosts focused discussions beyond the core Direct2Dell blogs to communicate with environmentally conscious customers, college recruits, and channel partners.

Dell has even established an "island" in the virtual world of Second Life.

Figure 5.2
Dell island in Second Life.

Southwest Airlines

Regardless of the current quality of a company's customer service, there are opportunities for improvement to be realized by "talking" one-on-one with customers using Twitter, blogs, or social networks. Southwest Airlines established its social media team to extend the touch points of the brand into the digital realm. They listen to conversations on Twitter, seeking opportunities to provide customer support. The team also includes staff who monitor a Facebook group, interact with bloggers, and review the company's presence on sites such as YouTube, Flickr, and LinkedIn. If someone posts a complaint in cyberspace, the company is ready to respond quickly.

General Motors

GM has a stable of seven blogs it uses to communicate directly with its customers around topics ranging from design to "green" technology. In addition to the blogs, GM uses Flickr to "share" high-quality images of its vehicles, photos from press events, and calendars featuring GM cars.

GM took advantage of the fact that Flickr's users already included a sizeable number of car enthusiasts who would be predisposed to sharing and commenting on the company's images. The company also has a number of channels on YouTube where it shares videos related to cars and car culture. By using existing networks for its content, GM saves money on infrastructure and takes advantage of the large numbers of users these networks have to offer.

Appropriately for a multinational company, GM has regional social media assets. The GM Europe blog, YouTube, webTV, and Flickr accounts are all linked and cross-referenced, with the company's European Social Media newsroom serving as a hub for its social media activities in the region.

Research In Motion (RIM)

RIM, best known for producing the BlackBerry phone, has an online BlackBerry Owner's Lounge. In the Lounge, BlackBerry members can voice their opinions through interactive polls, download productivity tools and games, and interact with other BlackBerry members. The site makes the BlackBerry more useful and compelling to its users. To take advantage of what's available, owners must register as community members, allowing the company to capture the email addresses and product registration information of its most passionate customers.

Workplace Collaboration for Engineering, R&D, Product Development, and General Productivity

We've already discussed how social media can be used to connect global workforces. Social collaboration tools such as wikis and blogs have freed many workers from the traditional fixed-location office. Software developers can share and edit code on private wikis. Researchers can gather and post data on a blog for peers in their field to review. Employees at a variety of organizations are finding innovative ways to enable people to meet and work together using social media.

Rosen Law

Rosen Law is a boutique North Carolina law firm specializing in divorce matters. Prior to investigating social media solutions for collaboration, the firm relied heavily on Lotus Notes to manage documents, email, calendars, and court schedules. Lee Rosen, chief executive and owner of the firm, wanted to find a way to get his employees to collaborate more effectively. He also wanted to move his firm away from Lotus Notes, which required a dedicated server and the services of an IT consultant for routine maintenance.

According to a February 2008 report on CNN Money, Rosen Law was spending about $25,000 on maintenance and additional licenses for new employees. Lee Rosen decided to move his company onto PBwiki, an internal collaboration tool. PBwiki costs the firm $600 per year. In addition to cost savings, Rosen cites usability as another benefit of the wiki:

> "The biggest reason that we're switching is that the wiki is easier to use," says Rosen. "If employees see a better way to organize or present information, they can just go ahead and do it with a wiki. With Lotus Notes, it required a programmer."

Canadian Airports Council

The Canadian Airports Council (CAC) is a trade association for Canada's airports. The CAC has 49 member organizations that represent more than 180 airports. Members of the CAC manage most of the nation's air cargo and passenger traffic, contributing to over $45 billion in economic activity in the communities they serve. They work with 5 other airport councils internationally, which consist of over 580 members operating over 1,647 airports in 175 countries.

With members scattered across the globe, the need to add transparency to collaborative work on proposals and documents arose. The council needed a more efficient way to enable collaboration and build on collective expertise.

In addition, discussions taking place over email had no visibility to anyone not copied, which made knowledge and information impossible to archive and cross-reference for use in the future by the broader group. With 9 main committees and 12 subcommittees all working on various proposals, transparency, and the management of all of the input on those documents, was a significant challenge.

CAC contemplated several options, ruling out SharePoint, which management felt was too document-centric. They went with a collaboration solution from Jive software called The Link. The Link combines wikis, blogs, discussion forums, and automated email notifications into a comprehensive and shared workspace.

Daniel-Robert Gooch, Director of Communications, cited The Link's usability as a factor that drove user adoption. The company also launched a communications campaign during the software's implementation and set up email notifications based on employee associations in committees to increase adoption and visibility. The Council now has instantaneous visibility of all discussions, ideas, and documents within and across committees.

Central Intelligence Agency (CIA)

In September 2008, the CIA launched a social network, named A-Space, for analysts to help 16 intelligence agencies share information. After logging in, analysts have access to shared and personal workspaces, wikis, blogs, widgets, RSS feeds, and other tools. Members of A-Space are prompted to fill out personal profiles and workspaces, detailing the projects they are working on. These networking features, similar to Facebook, help analysts seek out people working on similar issues and intelligence projects. For example, analysts in the state of New York are able to track critical intelligence-gathering efforts across the country in California.

Although, the CIA has embraced social networking and collaboration tools, they've still aligned A-Space with their stringent IT and security standards. To log in, analysts need to authenticate themselves using public key infrastructure (encryption), and their identities are checked against a government-wide intelligence analyst directory.

The CIA successfully embraced social media to spur employee collaboration while supporting its commitment to information security and standards.

Electronic Arts

With 9000 employees working at 18 locations in nine different countries, internal collaboration is critical to the success of video game developer and distributor Electronic Arts (EA). And with the majority of EA's people racing the clock to develop the next hot title, efficient cross-functional communications is key to the company's competitiveness in a dynamic market.

As many global corporations have found, collaboration can be difficult. EA made use of SharePoint and other collaboration tools in the past but found them limiting. They discovered that MySpace and Facebook contained enough information about a person to allow others to understand his or her role, experience, and job skills, so they chose to use these social networks instead of an internal database for that purpose. EA created an internal social networking tool called EA People to connect producers, artists, engineers, programmers, and so on, and give colleagues an engaging and easy window into what others were doing, allowing them to collaborate and share ideas, tools, and technologies with each other. EA's employee population skews to the younger side, and most are heavily involved in social media networks outside of the workplace, so this approach required no cultural adjustment by employees.

Prior to launching its online collaboration efforts, EA did many of the things most large companies do to foster better working relationships. The company ran global workshops aimed at solving business problems and discussing the company's strategic direction. Typically the game publisher brought in experts to solve problems and run workshops. The sense of community and collaboration at the workshops was invigorating, but once the workshops were finished, little of the spirit or lessons learned were retained. Bert Sandie, who leads Communities and Knowledge Management for EA, needed to find a way to keep those social interactions alive even after the workshops. He tried wikis and SharePoint but found they were not quite rich enough. Next he implemented forums, but they didn't allow employees to really get to know each other. Sandie looked to the success of social media networks like MySpace, and EA People grew out of that concept.

To identify the right kind of internal collaboration tool and network, Sandie had to ask the following questions: What are the daily interactions of employees? What are the best sharing tools, techniques, and processes? He recognized the key to these questions was in human interaction and social connection. Thusly, the foundation of EA People is, simply put, to give employees the ability to share everything. EA People's interface is rich in functionality and has search-able fields for expertise, job titles, an employee's place in the team hierarchy, photos, and so on, with links to each team member's profile page. Having this employee information easily accessible aids game innovation by making it easier to talk with peers and get a wider audience of EA experts to weigh in with ideas and suggestions. EA People allows everyone across the organization to interact, and the company is free to use and modify the platform any way they wish, with none of the intellectual property or privacy issues they would have using a third-party social networking application.

Interestingly, there's been no official requirement for employees to create pro-files in EA People, but employee adoption has been viral like any public social network. There's also been no official launch or announcement. Yet EA People is getting hundreds of new employee profile signups daily. Bert Sandie says EA's target is to get at least half of all employees to sign up.

A laid-back company like EA can't be too strict about any rollout, and EA has even used contests to help build excitement for the tool.

Sandie's observation is that this platform has started to humanize the corpora-tion, fuel innovation, and help management make better business decisions. EA's CEO even created his own profile in an effort to encourage all employees to add their own profiles.

The end goal of EA People is to improve the business process. EA believes social media is the way to achieve that goal in 2008.

Sabre Airline Solutions

Sabre provides technology solutions to the airline industry to optimize operations, costs, and management. Sabre Holdings runs most of the world's airline flight reservation systems. With more than 50 percent of their employees located outside the U.S., they launched a suite of social networking applications to help employees collaborate on business problems. The wider social network launched by the company was Sabre Town, an enterprise version of Facebook.

Sabre Town incorporates many of the features people have come to expect from any social network (whether for personal or business-related purposes). The profiles also provide detail around standard employee attributes such as contacts, skills, and expertise. The profiles are also heavy in personal data populated using casual questions about a user's hometown, favorite hobbies, and lunch spots.

Perhaps the most innovative feature of the network is its use of semantic technology and relevance engines (emerging search technologies that go beyond pattern matching to factor meaning, context, and the relationship between terms). The engine was developed using the company's proprietary software for predictive modeling and customer relationship management (CRM). On Sabre Town, users can post a question to the entire organization, and the site's relevance engine will automatically send the question to the 15 most relevant employees. Issues are forwarded to the most relevant parties and resolved quickly due to the intelligence and transparency of the tool. The incredible power of this feature alone has been credited with the swift and widespread adoption of Sabre Town.

Sixty-five percent of all Sabre employees became active members within the first three months. More than 90 percent of employees are active today.

Business Partners

Just as social media can be used to foster better collaboration between internal groups, these tools can be used to improve communications and efficient working relationships with business partners.

Xerox

Xerox is making creative use of social media to develop relationships with business partners associated with the company's principal business: document management. Xerox currently publishes nine blogs to address several of the company's core business-to-business (B2B) constituencies. For example, Lynette McTeague writes The Manufacturing Industry blog, highlighting current industry themes and challenges. She identifies opportunities for manufacturing organizations to use document-related concepts and technologies to reduce costs, improve client relationships, and increase productivity. Scott Titus writes the Ideas, Ideas, Ideas blog, which is a collection of his thoughts on marketing in the document management industry. Really is a blog that tracks Xerox's presence in the Second Life virtual world, where the company maintains both public and private (employee-only) spaces.

By emphasizing relevant, high-quality writing from recognized experts, Xerox succeeded in elevating its blog above hundreds of less inspirational examples. By keeping the company's core customers in mind, and going beyond marketing materials and press releases, Xerox makes good use of its blogs to position the company as a thought leader in document management technology.

HSBC

HSBC, one of the largest banks in the world, provides a comprehensive suite of financial services to its customers. The company serves a wide range of customers, including startups. Startup companies face a unique set of challenges that make for an incredibly low rate of survival beyond the five-year mark. HSBC started a local UK social network to connect entrepreneurs through the use of blogs, photo albums, videos, and forums.

There are currently over 375 member profiles on the network, and the average poll draws between 30 and 50 responses. The community is small yet incredibly active. For a global bank, this represents a small fraction of HSBC's business customers, but the success of this network will likely serve as a template for future social media initiatives.

Marketing

The use of social media in marketing is quite widespread and has been one of the earliest and most popular applications. Here are a couple of examples most notable for their success in going beyond marketing to engage customers in communities wherein they can share their ideas and learn from like-minded professionals and industry experts.

Lulu.com

Lulu provides content owners with the tools to publish and sell print-on-demand books, images, and calendars. Lulu has built a community of authors through the use of forums, newsletters, groups, and blogs. There are over 2,500 authors on Lulu's "Promote Your Book" group discussing plot lines and book promotion.

In addition to highlighting the benefits of their products and services in their blog, Lulu offers nontraditional book and music marketing strategies for money-strapped authors, musicians, and writers. For example, the Lulu Blog recently shared advice on how to use Twitter to promote a self-published work.

A Lulu blogger explained how Twitter works for a potential author:

> "I enjoy hockey and am working on a book about youth hockey, so I searched for 'hockey' and then followed other people who enjoy the sport. This has allowed me to join in on conversations with my target audience: hockey fans. As I have gotten to know them, I have been able to talk to them about ideas for my book, and even solicit feedback on some of my chapters. I know that once I release my book, I will have a built-in audience that is not only interested in my work but has also participated in its creation."

Visa

In June 2008, Visa launched a Facebook network application for small business owners. Articles and guides from sources like *The Wall Street Journal*, *Forbes*, and *Entrepreneur* were made available to members of the group. To drive user adoption, Visa awarded the first 20,000 U.S.-based businesses to join the Visa Business Network a $100 credit for free Facebook advertising.

With 1,954 fans, the Visa Business Network application on Facebook allows small business owners to find and exchange ideas with other business owners. They also have the option of creating Facebook profiles for their businesses in hopes that they will connect and share knowledge with other small business owners.

CASE STUDY

American Red Cross

The American Red Cross has an illustrious history of aiding in times of war and natural disaster. In its 125-year-plus history, the organization has developed a reputation for providing indispensible services at home and abroad. Like many public and private organizations, the Red Cross has recently had to develop new communications strategies in response to urban disasters of unprecedented devastation and scale. At the same time, the organization has experienced some loss of credibility for its handling of the Hurricane Katrina crisis. The Red Cross quickly established that social media would be important to solving both problems.

The American Red Cross was the largest single recipient of donations in response to the Hurricane Katrina crisis. The charity provided support in the form of food, supplies, and household products. But the organization's response to the hurricane drew criticism from its foreign counterparts, as well as victims and volunteers on the ground. The American Red Cross was accused of improper diversion of relief supplies; inadequate tracking and distribution of supplies; and the use of felons and severely unprepared volunteers as relief workers. An internal investigation was launched to rectify these problems, but the damage was done. The public perception of the American Red Cross declined, and negative conversations about the group found a home on the Internet.

The charity relies heavily on donations from the public, so the need to rebuild trust was critical. Managers at the organization determined that broad use of social media would be part of its plan to improve its standing in the public eye.

To encourage user adoption inside the organization, each office is commissioned with a blog and is required to make updates immediately on a disaster blog when a crisis strikes. Each storm has a dedicated WordPress blog (for example, http://hurricaneike.wordpress.com). The Red Cross also manages activities through Facebook and an organizational blog where internal contributors share stories of what they do on a day-to-day basis. Red Cross also makes use of social media newsrooms (see the sidebar "Social Media Newsrooms") to provide bloggers and reporters with a single, social media–enabled hub for all communications activities.

They've also been very successful in using Twitter for updating the public minute-by-minute as a disaster unfolds. Given that during a natural disaster people might not find themselves in front of a computer with an Internet connection, the Red

Cross social media strategy makes uses of cellular phone text messaging (SMS, or Short Message Service), in several ways. First, the organization encourages users with cell phones to check in "safe and well" by sending a text message:

The Red Cross also issues updates, including the locations of shelters, via Twitter, which users can receive on their cell phones. Finally, Red Cross personnel in the field use Utterli, a free service that lets users record audio updates from their cell phones that are automatically uploaded to a website and linked from Twitter.

The Red Cross understands the value of listening to and engaging in conversations regarding the organization as they arise in the blogosphere. Each day, the organization's Social Media team conducts searches on Twitter, Technorati, and Google for the Red Cross brand. The results are then aggregated into a daily "Blog Update" to 100 or more people in the Red Cross who respond when appropriate.

Figure 5.3
Red Cross "safe and well" check-in.

The Red Cross day-to-day involvement in thousands of communities around the country made the organization an ideal candidate for the kind of online communities social media can build. Prior to Katrina, the charity's leadership was slow to adopt social media, and they only "got into the game" when they were forced to rebuild trust in the wake of the groundswell of negative opinion that followed the organization's handling of Katrina. The Red Cross quickly realized that their failure to participate in conversations occurring in social media could leave their credibility and reputation vulnerable and unmanaged. The resulting success of social media for the American Red Cross has reinvigorated the organization and made it more responsive to public needs and a model for social media use in a crisis.

Social Media Newsrooms

Social media and Web 2.0 technologies are playing an increasingly important role in online communications, and companies of all sizes are looking for ways to use these technologies to better disseminate information.

A social media newsroom is an update on the traditional company website news page. The social media newsroom is built on a Web 2.0 foundation and offers all of the power and capability that implies, including speed, ease-of-use, tagging and sharing of content, RSS feeds, syndication for news distribution, and so on.

Although traditional websites still play a role in corporate communications, though arguably a diminished one, the static website cannot offer the ease of use and dynamic capabilities of a social media newsroom, such as the following:

o The ability to publish news almost instantaneously, without any knowledge of HTML, allows companies to make important announcements quickly and makes the site more timely and useful.

o The ability to easily include video, audio, and still images helps make the site livelier and more engaging and increases visitor time on the site.

o Tagging and bookmarking capabilities make it easier for people to find and share content.

o RSS feeds allow journalists to easily subscribe to customized company news feeds so that they can receive updates as they happen.

Following the 2008 announcement by the SEC that it would allow companies to use their social media–enabled websites to comply with the financial reporting requirements for publicly held companies, the social media newsroom could easily fulfill this requirement, freeing the company from the cost and lengthy process of traditional SEC financial reporting.

The social media newsroom is also a "Trojan horse" for introducing social media technology into a conservative organization that might not be ready for executive blogs or customer forums. With a social media newsroom, a company can gain familiarity with software implementation and use, etiquette, features, and power of social media with less perceived risk.

continues on next page

Social Media Newsrooms *(continued)*

Finally, particularly for companies that do not have executive blogs, the social media newsroom is an outstanding tool for crisis communications, allowing a company to respond instantaneously, and with high impact, in a demanding communications situation.

PR agencies and marketing firms are designing and implementing social media newsrooms for clients, and some clients are developing these newsrooms internally. Shift Communications has developed a social media newsroom template and has deployed its own social media newsroom. Eastwick Communications has deployed a social media newsroom on its own site, and with clients like Seagate Technology and myDIALS. SJ Communications and NewMediAwake have developed a social media newsroom for Virgin Megastores.

Much of the power of social media comes from the underlying technology—things like RSS feeds, tags, and rich media functionality (video and audio)—and these capabilities can help you post company news in a highly visible, shareable, engaging, and more effective way than your current website permits.

Many smaller companies choose to post their releases in a social media newsroom instead of using traditional news wires, or they may use the traditional news wires only occasionally, enjoying the ability to post an unlimited number of items on the social media newsroom. (Once you implement a social media newsroom there is no cost to post a news item other than a few minutes to write the item and publish it.) Not only will posting your own news reduce costs, it will give you pinpoint control over the format, look and feel, and publication schedule of your news.

Traditional HTML-based websites are largely invisible to thousands of people, like bloggers, online journalists, analysts, customers, organization members, and shareholders. The social media newsroom "behaves" a lot like a blog. The moment you post news to the social media newsroom, it is instantly disseminated across the web and around the globe and made available to millions of people.

Social Media Newsrooms *(continued)*

The social media newsroom is generally based on blogging software and administered through a simple, web-based editor, requiring no knowledge of HTML or other web technologies. Just enter a news item, add some tags, an image, a video, a link, and so on, and click "publish," and news is instantly posted to your website. What once took hours or days can now be done in minutes.

Electrolux (Sweden), GM Europe, and Cisco are among the dozens of large companies that have deployed social media newsrooms.

Figure 5.4
GM social media newsroom.

There are alternatives to the social media newsroom that offer many of the same benefits. Traditional news wires PR Newswire, BusinessWire, and Marketwire are adding social media capabilities to the press releases they distribute on behalf of clients. Although extra charges may apply for these services, the news wires have the distribution networks and infrastructure to allow your company to get into the social media news distribution game at the throw of a switch.

Marketwire and PR Newswire also have their own social media newsroom offerings. PRX Builder (with distribution through PR Newswire) and socialmedianewsroom.com offer companies a web-based DIY approach to social media news distribution. Communicators should also look into PitchEngine, which provides a unique community environment for building and sharing press releases and company news.

Balancing Social Media Risk and Reward

If at times this book appears to take a tentative or even cynical tone, it is because there are numerous risks *and* rewards involved in the adoption of social media. The purpose of this chapter is to explore some of these risks and offer suggestions on mitigating them through education and policy.

Many of the attributes of social media that make it so compelling in corporate communications, like speed and transparency, can also be a source of legal risk, ethical risk, and potential damage to the company's brand or reputation.

Ethical Issues in Corporate Social Media

An ethical company will always strive to behave ethically in every aspect of its business, but the area of emerging communications seems to have spawned a cornucopia of ethical missteps and some of the most interesting case studies in recent memory. I attend a monthly informal luncheon with Santa Cruz area public relations (PR) professional. We recently discussed social media, and agreed strongly that one of the worst things that could happen is for one of our clients to become a social media ethics case study.

Many communications professionals are familiar with stories of well-known companies using online media, either inadvertently or deliberately, to deceive consumers and investors. In 2007, Wal-Mart and Edelman PR received widespread attention for the "Wal-Marting Across America" flog (fake blog), which featured a couple traveling around the country in an RV, visiting Wal-Mart parking lots and rubbing elbows with the hoi polloi. Unfortunately, the couple turned out to be a professional journalist and photojournalist hired by Wal-Mart and Edelman.

And later in the year, John Mackey, the CEO of Whole Foods, attracted the attention of the Securities and Exchange Commission (SEC) and the Federal Trade Commission (FTC) when it was revealed that he was anonymously post-ing negative comments in Yahoo Finance forums in an alleged attempt to drive down the valuation of a company Whole Foods was in negotiations to acquire.

Unfortunately, many companies have been slow to learn from these exam-ples, and while these two stories are perhaps the most widely known, incidents of corporate social media deception continue. So why do large, ostensibly responsible corporations persist in trying to "game the system?"

In some ways, our capitalist system encourages deception because the forces applying pressures to achieve revenue and growth are rewarded more strongly than those encouraging ethical behavior. This may be a bit extreme, and your company is most likely a highly ethical one, but these pressures are very real, and even the most ethical people sometimes show very poor judg-ment when they are pushed hard to deliver difficult bottom-line results.

There are many deterrents to unethical online conduct. Most social media applications capture the unique IP address of every person posting a com-ment, making it easy for corporate IT departments and law enforcement to trace the origin of a comment. In other cases, persistent bloggers and con-sumers have detected, investigated, and reported ethical breaches.

Many of those who have been caught cheating claimed to be confused about the rules for using blogs and other social media in marketing and public relations. "This is unfamiliar territory," they protest. "We're on the frontier of communications. The rules are being written as we speak." Nice try. New media does not require new morality. Most of us know right from wrong, and just because a company is using a blog or an online forum doesn't release it from its responsibility for ethical behavior.

Nearly everyone can agree that stealing is wrong. (I say nearly, because I will allow that there are those who don't recognize the right to own property). The Koran, the Bible, and the Torah, for example, all have specific injunctions against stealing that are thousands of years old. Is it reasonable then to conclude that it's OK to take someone's iPhone, as these ancient laws could not possibly have foreseen the introduction of this product? Of course that's ludicrous. And it is no less ludicrous to say that social media is so new and mysterious that of course there will be missteps. When you deceive consumers, or when you misrepresent to inflate the worth of your company or its products and services, that's wrong.

Regulation Is Changing the Climate in Social Media Ethics

Companies are no longer basing social media ethics decisions solely on what "feels" right. Regulators are stepping in. The FTC already regulates unfair business and competitive practices, and the European Union's (EU) Unfair Commercial Practices Directive bars companies from certain deceptive practices. The EU has announced that it will apply this directive specifically to certain unethical social media practices, and new, more specific regulations (and accompanying penalties) are certainly in the works.

The risks to the corporation of pursuing strategies of questionable ethical intention are great. In Mackey's case, he invoked the ire of the SEC and the FTC—not a good thing to do as the CEO of a publicly held company. In the Wal-Mart case, the retailer's reputation, not very good to begin with, suffered a serious hit. And while so far most penalties have been nonfinancial, the shroud of mystery surrounding social media is starting to lift, so you can expect legislators and regulators to start going after more companies who try to play the "wild, wild west" card. While Mackey and his communications team still claim mitigating circumstances, a 16-word comment on Mackey's blog indicates that some people see things differently:

> "A corporate officer anonymously posting about their own company and their competitors. Seems unethical to me."

So how do you avoid the ethical pitfalls presented by emerging communications? Behave ethically. Hire ethical people. Make ethical decisions. Implement clear policies and ensure companywide understanding of, and agreement to, those policies. Provide training on proper social media practice and ethics. Develop a social media code of ethics. Review and adopt the ethical guidelines offered by major industry associations like the Word of Mouth Marketing Association (www.womma.org), the Public Relations Society of America (www.prsa.org), and the International Association of Business Communicators (www.iabc.com).

And the next time you're in a meeting and someone proposes some bonehead initiative that might push the ethical envelope, protect the interests of the company and take an ethical stand.

Social Media Ethics Made Easy

It should come as no surprise that certain social media tactics are unethical and/or illegal. While more specific regulation regarding social media seems to be required, the basic laws and ethical traditions against misrepresentation, unfair competitive practices, deceit, and so on have been in place for hundreds of years.

The Constitution does not permit falsehoods or deceptions in speech, which includes any form of public communications, when they may jeopardize the public good. Oliver Wendell Holmes, Jr. said, when interpreting the First Amendment in Schenck v. United States:

> "The most stringent protection of free speech would not protect a man in falsely shouting fire in a theater and causing a panic."

We also have specific laws in the commercial sector against making misrepresentations of things like product superiority or company financial performance. These laws are designed to protect consumers, and we know from the excesses and outright theft perpetrated by Enron and others during the dotcom bust, that such protections are necessary.

Increasingly, companies that fail to understand the social media landscape, and that engage in ill-conceived initiatives or random acts of communication, will run afoul of regulators and may find themselves charged with civil and legal violations. The line between legal and ethical violations often blurs, as naturally many forms of conduct can violate both standards. And in turn, legal and ethical violations almost always lead to damage to the company's reputation, if not its failure altogether. (No one wants his or her company to be the next Enron.)

Existing U.S. Legislation

Though it may not be necessary to say so, one of the easiest steps you can take toward ensuring legal compliance in your company's social media initiatives is to acquaint yourself with established laws that apply to the company's existing online communications. In general, any law or regulation that applies to any communications on your company's website, can be assumed to apply equally to any external social media initiative.

It is very important that you involve the company's investor relations, legal, and finance organizations in the development of social media policy and procedures. Investor relations and finance should also be permitted to review all company social media content relevant to financial disclosure, including executive blog posts, prior to posting.

Perhaps the three most important and well-known sources of regulatory oversight are the Securities and Exchange Commission (SEC), the Federal Trade Commission (FTC), and for companies doing business internationally, the European Union (EU).

SEC

The SEC is the principal U.S. government agency responsible for regulating the communication of financial information by publicly held companies. The SEC also regulates some aspects of investor communications in companies that are not publicly held. As previously mentioned, the safest assumption is that all SEC regulations that affect the company's website and other online activities also apply to any social media initiatives.

Regulation Full Disclosure (Reg FD) is the SEC regulation governing full and fair disclosure of financial information for publicly held companies. Reg FD governs reporting methods, frequency, quiet periods, and so on, and publicly traded companies must manage communications carefully to avoid running afoul of the SEC.

On July 30, 2008, in a breakthrough ruling, the SEC approved the use of company websites for the distribution of information in compliance with Reg FD. The SEC, and chairman Christopher Cox, are to be applauded for bringing the agency into the 21st century so boldly.

Excerpts from the SEC's 2008 Announcement

"Today we are recommending that the Commission issue an interpretive release to provide additional guidance and greater certainty on how companies can use their websites to provide information to investors in compliance with the federal securities laws, particularly with respect to the Securities Exchange Act of 1934."

The announcement goes on to outline those situations in which companies may use their public websites to comply with:

"...Regulation FD and satisfaction of Regulation FD's 'public disclosure' requirement. In evaluating whether information is 'public' for purposes of the applicability of Regulation FD to subsequent discussions or disclosure, companies must consider whether and when:

o A company website is a recognized channel of distribution

o Posting of information on a company website disseminates the information in a manner making it available to the securities marketplace in general; and

o There has been a reasonable waiting period for investors and the market to react to the posted information.

...Finally, the release acknowledges that the nature of online information is increasingly interactive, and not static. The release, therefore, makes clear that information appearing on company websites does not need to satisfy a printer-friendly standard or be in a format comparable to paper-based information, unless the Commission's rules explicitly require it."

FTC

The FTC has extensive laws and regulations governing commerce—online and offline. The FTC's Title 16—Commercial Practices includes rules on many aspects of fair business practices that might arise on a blog, customer forum, or online newsroom, such as:

- Pricing practices
- General consumer privacy
- Online privacy for children

- Endorsements

- Use of the word *free*

The FTC also has separate acts that may affect you, including The Children's Online Privacy Protection Act, and the organization is extremely active in protecting against identity theft and fighting spam.

Like SEC regulations, it is reasonable and prudent to assume that all FTC rules apply to both conventional website activities as well as social media initiatives. Since it is beyond the scope of this book to provide a comprehensive education in compliance with all FTC regulations, it is recommended that you visit the FTC website and work closely with your legal department to understand all the FTC regulations that might affect your social media initiatives.

EU Directives

The European Union's Unfair Commercial Practices Directive enacted in May, 2005, bars companies from "falsely claiming or creating the impression that the trader is not acting for purposes relating to his trade, business, craft or profession, or falsely representing oneself as a consumer" which covers *astroturfing* (see the sidebar "Social Media Ethics Terms") and other social media sins. EU regulations affect all companies doing business in the EU, regardless of the location of the company's headquarters.

Pending U.S. Legislation

In March, 2007, Kentucky Representative Tim Couch introduced HB 775, a bill "to establish definitions relating to Internet websites, blogs, or message boards; require registration prior to posting information to these interactive services; identify persons, businesses, or entities that post information to these interactive services; establish penalty provisions."

The bill would require anyone who contributes to a website to register their real name, address, and email address with that site. Their full name would be used any time a comment is posted. If the bill becomes law, the website operator would have to pay if someone was allowed to post anonymously on their site. The fine would be $500 for a first offense and $1,000 for each offense after that.

There are sure to be many additional bills proposed, and eventually enacted, that will affect corporate social media activities.

Social Media Ethics Terms

Astroturfing

Astroturfing is an attempt to falsify a grassroots consumer movement through deceptive means. The term originated in politics and was coined by Senator Lloyd Bentsen. In social media, astroturfing usually manifests itself when people post positive comments about a company on blogs and in online communities without revealing that they are employees and/or representatives of the company. In some cases companies hire third parties, such as public relations agencies, to engage in astroturfing. Another form of astroturfing is the practice of hiring evangelists who chat favorably about a company on various social networks without revealing their affiliations. The European Union has outlawed the practice.

Blogola

The term *blogola* comes from the radio term *payola*, which originated in the 1950s. In its original usage, payola occurred when record company executives paid DJs to play certain songs and to "talk up" particular artists and records.

In the social media world, blogola typically describes a situation in which a blogger is given free merchandise, often with a request that the blogger review the product. Sometimes this request implies a favorable review in exchange for a "free" product.

Many blogola situations did not begin as deceptions. Mommy blogging, for example, began as an informal way for moms to blog about child raising techniques, nutrition, health, product safety, education, and other topics relevant to other mothers. Manufacturers of relevant products approached these bloggers with requests for product reviews. With the staggering growth of blogging in general, and mommy blogging in particular, what might have started out as a hobby blog, has for some mothers turned into a full-time profession, and in some cases quite a lucrative one, so the ethical standards that might have applied in the "early days" might no longer apply.

Many bloggers have in fact discontinued accepting free merchandise, choosing instead to return all review products to the manufacturer. In some areas this is more difficult than it sounds. For example, a reviewer cannot return food and wine. This can also be an issue in the travel industry, where many professional writers pay their own way but amateurs cannot afford to do so.

Social Media Ethics Terms *(continued)*

Brandjacking

Brandjacking is a relatively new term used to describe a situation when a person or company "hijacks" the brand identity of another company. This could include the unauthorized use of the company name, logos, product photography, product names, and even website URLs. Several corporate accounts on Twitter, for example, have turned out to be bogus. This is one of the more blatant forms of brandjacking, in which a person claims to be an official representative of the company.

Another milder form, which occurs often on Facebook, is the unauthorized use in an online discussion group or forum of the company's brand identity by an individual or group. In many cases, this occurs on "fan" pages and groups created by people who are enthusiastic about the company and its products. If the discussions in the group are largely favorable to the company, it may choose not to police this activity, even when it may constitute a violation of copyright or trademark law.

Comment Spam

Comment spammers attack blogs and online communities by leaving often innocuous-appearing comments that link to third-party sites. Comment spam is predominantly practiced by companies selling pornography, online gaming, and treatments for erectile dysfunction, so it is obviously something companies don't want on their websites. Most blogging software provides filtering for comment spam, and by moderating comments, you can keep comment spam off your blog and other social media sites.

Flog

A *flog* is a fake blog designed to deceive consumers and others by simulating a situation or story favorable to a company. Probably the best known flog is "Wal-Marting Across America," in which an "average couple" traveled the U.S. in an RV touring Wal-Mart parking lots and writing about their experiences on their blog. The couple turned out to be a professional photographer and professional journalist hired by Wal-Mart and its agency, Edelman, to write the blog.

continues on next page

Social Media Ethics Terms *(continued)*

A flog, which maliciously deceives to promote the company and its products, should not be confused with a parody blog, such as the Fake Steve Jobs blog, which was open about its artifice and intended strictly for entertainment purposes.

Link Baiting

Link baiting is perhaps one of the grayer areas of social media ethics, and some would argue that it is not unethical at all. Link baiting is the act of engaging in controversial conversation or running some kind of promotion that is intended to generate links to the site. Some of these are as blatant as offers of a cash reward randomly given to anyone who links to a particular site during a particular period of time.

Other approaches are more subtle. A blog post titled "Blogs Are Worthless" might generate a lot of traffic because it is a fairly outrageous statement coming from a blogger. Some would see this controversial point of view as link baiting, and others would see it simply as good marketing for the blog.

Principally, people are bothered by link baiting because the number of links to a site is a key metric affecting where that site will be placed in search results, and therefore the link baiting strategy is generally intended not to make the site more interesting or relevant but to fool Internet search engines and increase advertising revenue on sites that feature advertising.

Pay Per Post

Under a *pay per post* arrangement, a blogger is paid a flat rate per post to publish favorable posts about a company's products and services. Drawing its name from payperpost.com, pay per post is another form of blogola, as Michael Arrington wrote on his TechCrunch blog, "How Much Is Your Soul Worth? PayPerPost Now Lets Bloggers Set The Price." Pay per post creates confusion among readers as they are generally unaware that the blog they are reading is essentially sponsored by a company that might seem to be receiving objective coverage on the blog.

Social Media Ethics Terms *(continued)*

Screen Scraping

Screen scraping is the use of technology to "scrape" content from a blog or website and to republish it on another site without permission. Scraping may violate trademark and copyright protections, and it is also specifically prohibited by the user agreements of many websites and social networks. Screen scraping is so named because instead of using the data output by a program or output from an RSS feed, screen scraping copies, pixel by pixel, the information as displayed on the screen.

Splog

A *splog*, or spam blog, is a spurious blog set up to capture search engine results and divert them to other blogs or websites. The articles are bogus, sometimes using nonsensical text and other times using text specially developed to improve search engine rankings.

Risk Mitigation

There are many ways to mitigate the risk that may be posed by social media initiatives in your company. Key among these is education. Be aware of the law, and keep up with social media ethics case studies and resources like the ones in this chapter.

Any company with a sound legal and ethical foundation in general should have no trouble behaving legally and ethically in its social media initiatives.

While it's beyond the scope of this book to design a comprehensive, company-wide legal and ethics compliance program, the following sections offer some suggestions for ensuring compliance with the company's standards.

Social Media Education

Social media education can come in many forms. Many organizations hold social media conferences and offer both in-person and web-based social media education programs. You can of course develop your own programs in-house, which would allow you to customize your curriculum.

There are also hundreds of social media get-togethers around the world every month, most free and open to the public.

Many companies also schedule regular social media get-togethers in-house, in which employees who are involved in social media policymaking, selection and implementation of software and tools, or are simply heavy users of social media, meet on a regular basis to talk about new tools, ethics, social media strategy, and so on. These can be made more interesting and more relevant with the inclusion of external speakers with expertise on these topics. Some companies choose to do these get-togethers after hours, on campus, and may invite the general public to attend. This is a great way for your employees to network with others outside your company who are involved in corporate social media.

Facebook Fridays at Sun Microsystems

Sumaya Kazi, Senior Media Manager of Sun Microsystems Global Communications division, organized "Sun Facebook Fridays" at Sun as a way for Sun employees and social media enthusiasts to get together on a weekly basis to discuss social media. The group is described on its Facebook page as:

o A group brought to you by Sun Microsystems and dedicated to connecting those interested in learning more and staying on top of Social Media news.

o A weekly Friday Social Media e-Newsletter with a lot of must-have goodies (interesting stats, facts, people, articles, info, and updates on Social Media activities in play).

o A quick way to become a mini–Social Media guru. You can now be a great conversation starter at holiday parties. 100% Guaranteed.

o An opportunity to ask and get answers to your burning Social Media questions.

o A way to be empowered to brainstorm, connect with others, and launch innovative social media ideas.

Rules of engagement:

o Be an active reader.

o Share the knowledge.

o Invite others to the group.

o Give feedback.

Sun Facebook Fridays is very popular, with over 1,800 members. It averages 50–100 new members each week. It was recently opened to public participation and is available at www.facebook.com/sunfacebookfridays.

Social Media Usage Rules

It's critical in a company of any size to let employees know the company's rules and expectations for legal and ethical conduct. In most cases the company's standards of business conduct and/or employee handbook outline nearly all the expectations the company has of its employees, without, however, specifically spelling out social media. One mistake many people make is to assume that because social media is *new* there are somehow intricate new rules and regulations that might apply, or that the ethical standards might somehow be unclear. In general, this isn't true. The kinds of things called out in your company's standards of business conduct, like compliance with the law, prohibitions against disclosing company secrets, rules regarding financial disclosure, and other legal and ethical guidelines apply across the company to all employees, regardless of whether they are using social media.

However, since there does seem to be some confusion, it is often helpful, along with social media education programs, to develop specific social media policies, agreements, and codes of ethics, so that employees and members of the general public are aware of your standards for legal and ethical behavior. The next sections discuss a few of these documents.

Social Media Policies

A good social media policy will create a better informed group of social media users at the company, who will better represent the company and will not subject it to undue risk from inappropriate disclosure of financial information and proprietary company information, or from engaging in unfair business or competitive practices.

To design an effective social media policy that will be widely embraced and will achieve its intent, consider the following:

- Develop a comprehensive policy that extends to all employees and all use of social media and social networks whenever there is potential for employees to be seen as company representatives.

- Engage all appropriate organizations within the company, such as legal, finance, and marketing, when developing the policy.

- Be emphatic about the need for social media users to behave ethically, legally, and in the best interests of the company, its customers, employees, shareholders, and business partners.

Incorporate the company's culture in the policy. Avoid creating a burdensome policy that would limit the authenticity and effectiveness of your social media programs

Your social media policy is an extension of the company's standards of business conduct and reminds people that they represent the company in everything they do and should always act in good faith. Employees are entitled to have a private life and private use of social media, but when they are talking about anything that might relate to the company's business, or when it is clear they are affiliated with the company, they should understand the company's expectations when blogging, posting comments, using social networks, and so forth.

An overly burdensome policy will limit participation in social media programs, discourage new participants, slow the communications process, and add cost (for things like reviews and rewrites). Ultimately, the wrong social media policy could so limit the effectiveness of the company's social media programs as to make them not worth doing.

Codes of Ethics

There are several good codes of ethics and other guidelines that can be useful in establishing your company's social media policies. These are available from the Public Relations Society of America (PRSA), the International Association of Business Communicators (IABC), the Blog Council, the Word of Mouth Marketing Association (WOMMA), and other organizations.

Many companies use two versions of the code of ethics: a longer more formal version as a reference, and a shorter version published on the company's website offering full transparency to consumers and journalists regarding the company's ethical standards.

THE BLOG COUNCIL BEST PRACTICES TOOLKIT

The Blog Council has developed a "Disclosures Best Practices Toolkit," available at their website, www.blogcouncil.org, which addresses:

- Disclosure of identity
- Personal/unofficial blogging and outreach
- Blogger relations
- Compensation and incentives

- Agency and contractor disclosure

- Creative flexibility

As mentioned, many companies have both a long-form and short-form code of ethics. The long form is the *official* company social media code of ethics, and the short form is useful on the company's website blog and other online properties.

SHORT-FORM CODE OF ETHICS

The following is an example of a short-form code of ethics for use on a blog or website. This example reflects a particular company's personality, so it may not be suitable as-is for all companies. Like all policies, adoption and success are largely dependent on an understanding and reflection of the company's culture.

- We will write openly and honestly, on relevant topics about which we are knowledgeable and passionate.

- We will not embrace controversy simply to drive traffic to our site, nor will we shy away from it when it is called for.

- We will credit others and clearly indicate when we're using quoted material.

- We will not unfairly disparage our competitors in any way.

- We will respect the privacy of our customers, employees, business partners, and others we work with.

- We will disclose all affiliations in order to avoid any opportunity for misunderstandings as to our allegiances.

- We will keep original posts intact, indicating corrections, strikeouts, and other changes made after the original publication of the information.

- We will quickly and forthrightly acknowledge and correct all errors.

- Comments on this site are moderated, meaning they are held for review prior to publication. We will publish all comments provided they are even slightly relevant and are not obscene, profane or unduly inflammatory, and do not violate legal or ethical standards. We may elect not to respond to a comment on our site when that comment is irrelevant, or if a response might require the disclosure of inappropriate information such as company confidential information, financial information, and so on.

The WOMMA Ethics Code

The following is an excerpt from the WOMMA code:

1. Consumer protection and respect are paramount.

We respect and promote practices that abide by an understanding that the consumer not the marketer—is fundamentally in charge, in control, and dictates the terms of the consumer-marketer relationship. We go above and beyond to ensure that consumers are protected at all times.

2. The Honesty ROI: Honesty of Relationship, Opinion, and Identity

Honesty of Relationship

o We practice openness about the relationship between consumers, advocates, and marketers. We encourage word of mouth advocates to disclose their relationship with marketers in their communications with other consumers. We don't tell them specifically what to say, but we do instruct them to be open and honest about any relationship with a marketer and about any products or incentives that they may have received.

o We stand against shill and undercover marketing, whereby people are paid to make recommendations without disclosing their relationship with the marketer.

o We comply with FTC regulations that state: "When there exists a connection between the endorser and the seller of the advertised product which might materially affect the weight or credibility of the endorsement (for example, the connection is not reasonably expected by the audience) such connection must be fully disclosed."

Honesty of Opinion

o We never tell consumers what to say. People form their own honest opinions, and they decide what to tell others. We provide information, we empower them to share, and we facilitate the process—but the fundamental communication must be based on the consumers' personal beliefs.

o We comply with FTC regulations regarding testimonials and endorsements, specifically: "Endorsements must always reflect the honest opinions, findings, beliefs, or experience of the endorser. Furthermore, they may not contain any representations which would be deceptive, or could not be substantiated if made directly by the advertiser."

The WOMMA Ethics Code *(continued)*

Honesty of Identity

o Clear disclosure of identity is vital to establishing trust and credibility. We do not blur identification in a manner that might confuse or mislead consumers as to the true identity of the individual with whom they are communicating, or instruct or imply that others should do so.

o Campaign organizers should monitor and enforce disclosure of identity. Manner of disclosure can be flexible, based on the context of the communication. Explicit disclosure is not required for an obviously fictional character, but would be required for an artificial identity or corporate representative that could be mistaken for an average consumer.

o We comply with FTC regulations regarding identity in endorsements that state: "Advertisements presenting endorsements by what are represented, directly or by implication, to be 'actual consumers' should utilize actual consumers, in both the audio and video or clearly and conspicuously disclose that the persons in such advertisements are not actual consumers of the advertised product."

o Campaign organizers will disclose their involvement in a campaign when asked by consumers or the media. We will provide contact information upon request.

WOMMA Ethics Code reprinted with permission. www.womma.org/ ethics/code/read/

Sample Social Media Agreement

The intent of the social media agreement is to ensure that all employees are made aware of and agree to their responsibilities in complying with the company's standards of business conduct, code of ethics, and all laws and regulations that might affect their use of social media.

On pages 131–132 is a sample social media agreement. This document would be signed by all employees. It does not supersede the employee handbook and standards of business conduct. It is an internal company document. Social media agreements typically cover both company-sanctioned social media such as the company's blogs and online forums, as well as employee use of external social media such as social networks and chat rooms. Typically the company's standards of business conduct, which should be referenced in the social media agreement, provide guidelines for appropriate employee conduct in all matters in which they might be seen as company representatives. These guidelines often extend beyond the workday and the four walls of the company, as employees are expected to represent the company in good faith at all times.

You may feel free to use any or all of the following agreement, but you should review it with legal council before asking employees to sign it.

Sample Social Media Agreement

In order to ensure that the Company adheres to its ethical and legal obligations, the Employee is required to sign and comply with the Company's Social Media Agreement. The intent of this Agreement is not to restrict the flow of useful and appropriate information, but to limit risk to the Company's reputation, and legal and ethical standing.

This Agreement is intended to clearly define social media and its use. However, please note that as the field of social media is a rapidly changing one, and new tools and technologies may come into use, the same standards still apply, regardless of whether these new tools and technologies have been specifically named in the Agreement.

Definitions

For the purposes of this Agreement, social media is defined to include, but is not necessarily limited to, any of the following:

o Blogs

o Chat rooms

o Online forums

o Social networks like Facebook, Twitter, and MySpace

o Video sites like YouTube

Employee Use of Social Media

While employed at the Company, it is typical that the Employee might have the opportunity to create, publish, and share content using these and other online tools. This content could be published in the form of a blog posts, comments on blog posts, participation in discussions on online forums, biographical information in an online user profile, a "user generated" video or still image, or other content treated by the Employee and published online.

This Agreement covers both the use of Company sponsored social media, such as the Company's blog and customer forums, as well as the use of any general, public social media not sponsored by the Company, in which the Employee's name and/or affiliation with the Company may be in any way identifiable.

continues on next page

Sample Social Media Agreement *(continued)*

Supplements Existing Employee Agreements

Employee understands that the social media agreement supplements but does not supersede the Company's standards of business conduct, employee manual, or any other agreements the employee may have entered into with the Company.

The Company's standards of business conduct outline rules for appropriate representation of the Company, for personal ethical behavior as to how Employees conduct themselves in the public eye. The provisions of the standards of business conduct, including prohibitions against disclosing proprietary Company information, maintaining one's best efforts on behalf of the Company, and generally conducting oneself in an ethical way so as not to compromise the Company's reputation and standing in the marketplace, apply equally to any use of social media.

Prohibited Subjects

In order to maintain the company's reputation and legal standing, the following subjects may not be discussed by Employees in any form of social media:

o Company confidential or proprietary information

o Embargoed information such as launch dates, release dates, and pending reorganizations

o Company intellectual property such as drawings, designs, software, and patent applications

o Disparagement of company's or competitors' products, services, executive leadership, strategy, and business prospects

o Graphic sexual references

o References to illegal drugs

o Obscenity or profanity

o Disparagement of any race, religion, gender, sexual orientation, or place of national origin

Employee hereby agrees to comply with the terms of this Agreement, and understands that failure to do so may result in disciplinary action up to and including dismissal. *[Signature block]*

Can You Count Everything That Counts?

One of the most challenging aspects of social media is determining valid measures for success. Einstein said,

> "...not everything that can be counted counts, and not everything that counts can be counted,"

and nowhere is this more true than it is in social media measurement.

The value a company places on its social media initiatives will largely be based on its expectations. Although social media has been available to corporate communicators for several years, the field is still young enough that the debate over whether one can effectively measure social media impact is an ongoing one.

There are many, many measures that could apply, both qualitative and quantitative, and within each of these, the approach to gathering information varies as well. Currently, the most accurate and easily obtained measures will gauge campaign/initiative reach and adoption and will not extend to the measurement of *business* success metrics like revenue and lead generation.

In some cases, corporate communicators can employ publicly available websites and other tools to manually gather information. Many of the traditional measures of online marketing effectiveness apply quite easily to social media. These include such things as site traffic, search engine placement, number of links to the site, and so on.

Online Metrics

It's fairly simple to ascertain things like the number of visitors to a site, growth in that number over time, and the number of people who subscribe to a particular news feed; the number of times a video has been viewed; the number of comments received on the company's blog; and the number of members and discussions within the company's online communities. In many cases, there is a dashboard built into the administrative function of each social media application that will provide this data in an aggregated form, or it can be manually gathered.

Most companies will want more sophisticated data. There are many methods available for gathering this information, ranging from free online tools to enterprise-grade automated measurement tools.

Messaging Effectiveness

As in any form of communications, another measure of social media impact is messaging *uptake*, the degree to which the company's messages reach others, are republished, and are evaluated. A social media version of the traditional *coverage report* typically generated in public relations can be used to assess external message pickup. Many of the popular tools for finding the information for this kind of report are covered in "The Tools" section later in this chapter.

Measuring Social Media Business Objectives

As mentioned previously, social media initiatives, like all marketing and communications efforts, should be tied to business objectives. Doing so will make measurement easier.

For example, if the purpose of online community is to attract new developers, basic web analytics make it simple to see how many people clicked a link to register as a new developer, and the developer organization can tell you how many completed the registration process. It's also easy to see how many people downloaded a particular piece of software or a white paper, or subscribed to receive an email newsletter or other form of ongoing communication. These are just a few of the many situations in which the company automatically captures simple information about the people who visit online.

Limiting Interference with the User Experience

Some mechanisms for capturing this information, however, can be an impediment to reaching your audience. How many times, for example, have you clicked a link to an article only to find that a subscription is required before you can read the article? Even if the subscription is free, our time and our personal information are not, and we will often click the Back button, looking for another, less complicated source of the same information. People also hesitate to subscribe or register because of privacy concerns, and in reality, before online communications, when did we require people to tell us who they were before we marketed to them? True, even print publications like newspapers and magazines (and their advertisers) place a very high value on readership numbers and demographic profile, but you can pick up a copy of the magazine at the store, or if you don't mind it being seven years old, at the dentist's office, and read both the "paid" subscriber content as well as all the advertising without telling anyone who you are.

Remember, we're looking at social media in a business context, from the standpoint of a potential customer. There are many ways in which someone might learn about your blog, video podcast series, community, and so on. Perhaps a friend has shared a link, or more likely, they found you through a Google search as they were doing online research on a product for a personal or work-related purchase. People are on a mission to gather the greatest amount of relevant information as quickly as possible, and they will often not take the time to complete a registration form just to get past some annoying introductory page to view the information they came for.

For this reason, people who want to measure social media, and to be fair, nearly all online marketing, can use other less awkward methods to determine who they are reaching, in what numbers, and what those people are doing once they've been reached.

Behavior "after the search" is the most important measure of any online campaign. Did the reader, for example, visit the company's blog, and as a result, engage in some kind of behavior useful to the company? Did he or she make a purchase? This is probably the most important question and generally the most difficult to answer. Even on a site equipped to do e-commerce, registration is generally not required until the consumer decides to make the purchase, so the company can't always connect the purchase with a particular communications program or imitative. We've all been asked "How did you hear of us?" when making an online purchase, but this is anecdotal and not very reliable, and again, can be annoying to someone who just wants to buy a pair of shoes and move on.

Using a Microsite to Measure Campaign Effectiveness

Although there are few foolproof methods for tracking online behavior from initial search and discovery to revenue, there are a few that can provide valuable insights. One approach is the microsite, a special website, blog, or other online vehicle devoted to a specific product and/or promotion. Consumer businesses, for example, could launch a microsite tied to any of the dozens of seasonal promotions companies typically launch. A back-to-school microsite could use both established company branding and an event- or promotion-specific look and feel, and it could be targeted to specific demographics such as teenagers. Traffic to the site could be generated through social media and viral campaigns. These campaigns would have unique tracking URLs to identify the source of the visitors. Those who come to the site, and then elect to purchase, could be directed to a front-end ordering process separate from the process used on the main company website, thereby establishing a direct link between the social media and viral campaigns, and revenue.

Influence, Brand, Engagement, and Public Relations Value of Social Media

In addition to direct business measures, which are arguably the most important, there are other ways in which social media can positively affect your company and ways to measure that impact. These include the ability to influence important people, such as consumers and journalists; the ability to positively affect perceptions of the company's brand; the value social media offers through enhanced consumer engagement; and the public relations value of social media.

Influence

Influence is clearly a powerful force in social media but one that is hard to measure. Some social media pundits have proposed return on influence (obviously an attempt to re-spin the better known ROI—return on investment) as a specific measure of social media effectiveness, but we're a long way from "cracking the code" in terms of making this a reliable and consistent metric.

The influence concept is summed up nicely by the title of Jon Berry and Ed Keller's 2003 book, *The Influentials: One American in Ten Tells the Other Nine How to Vote, Where to Eat, and What to Buy.* Jay Deragon, one of the co-authors of *The Emergence of the Relationship Economy: The New Order of Things to Come*, wrote on his blog:

> "The social web is creating a reversal in the process of managing customers. People learn from people and subsequently are avoiding influence from institutions rather (than) the conversations of people, one to one to millions, have become the power of influence."

As social media becomes more and more mainstream, there is a growing network effect of staggering proportions that can be achieved through influence. Consider Facebook, for example, which currently claims over 100 million active users. If a consumer has a positive experience with a company, or becomes aware of someone else having such an experience by visiting a blog or through word-of-mouth, they might be inclined to share this on Facebook, thus reaching potentially 100 million people. In reality if I share something on Facebook, it reaches only my "friends," the people who are in my network, but they may pass the information on to their friends, and so on.

The sharing effect extends beyond the boundaries of a given social network. For example, Friendfeed, an aggregator of social network activity, can take information shared on Twitter and publish it as a Facebook status update, dramatically increasing the potential number of readers for a particular piece of information.

One comment or update could easily reach thousands or tens of thousands of people this way. We know this goes on, but no one has figured out how to simply and inexpensively perform the complex web forensics required to document the origin of many of these downstream communications.

This is just one of the many ways in which social media clearly has powerful business value that is highly difficult to measure. Again, the same could be said of nearly any marketing effort, so social media is not unique in this respect. When you go to the store and choose to pick up a can of Coke versus Pepsi, for example, that is a preference built on years and years of experience with the company, its products, and its brand. Who can say which of the company's marketing initiatives led to that purchase? In fact, maybe they all did.

Brand

In addition to driving purchasing decisions, most marketing and communications initiatives shape consumer perceptions. Social media can position the company as intelligent, connected, or even simply hip and cool. And while not every social media initiative should have "making the company look cool" as its primary goal, this is actually a valid business and communications objective for some companies.

The largest companies have significant brand equity, calculated by very complex formulae, measured in the billions of dollars and reflected on the company's balance sheet. Brand consultancy Interbrand publishes an annual survey of the most valuable global brands. According to the 2008 survey the five top global brands are: Coca Cola, IBM, Microsoft, GE, and Nokia

Number one, Coca Cola, has a brand valuation of nearly $67 billion. Effective marketing and communications are key among the factors that drive consumer brand perception and therefore value, and clearly, social media can play a significant role in this. And again, like nearly every section of this chapter, there is the caveat that this is difficult to directly measure.

Through surveys and focus groups and many of the metrics discussed here, there are downstream measures that can help you understand the impact of social media on the company's brand. At the end of the year, if a company's brand value has increased, that is certainly a measure of success, assuming your social media campaigns achieved their numeric goals and had a positive effect.

Due in part to the novelty of social media, there is also a secondary brand effect achieved through successful initiatives. Many consumers, journalists, and bloggers respect companies that employ social media and perceive them as being more progressive and more creative than more traditional companies.

Engagement

Another more ephemeral measure of social media success is what is referred to as *engagement*. The notion of engagement says that there is value to companies in making customers feel as if they are truly participating in a two-way conversation with the company; that is, they feel they have a voice within the company, that the company cares about them as individuals and listens and responds to what they have to say.

Maybe your CEO has an excellent blog and quickly and effectively responds to comments posted on the blog. A consumer who posts a question may feel as if he or she is "engaged in a conversation" with the CEO. For that particular consumer this can be a rewarding experience, and if properly managed by the CEO, can create a customer for life. But does this scale? How does the CEO reach millions, when directly reaching a hundred a year would be an aggressive goal?

Engagement does scale, in a hard to measure but nonetheless very real way. Anyone who reads the blog or subscribes to it via a news reader, will be aware of these exchanges, even if they didn't personally participate. The fact that the CEO is behaving in a transparent and highly visible way demonstrates the company's interest in its customers.

Basic web metrics, like the number of visitors to your social media sites, what they read once they get there, and how long they are there, are very important to understanding the direct impact of these conversations. In addition to reaching direct readers of the CEO's blog, there is an added impact created by those who have had the opportunity to interact one-on-one with the CEO of a large company and choose to use social networks and blogs to share that experience with their friends and colleagues. And since these interactions are on the company's public website, and "visible" to search engines, there is a public record of the CEO's conduct easily found by anyone doing a web search on the company.

Many journalists and bloggers read executive blogs to see what an executive is up to and to monitor the trend and tone of these conversations to gauge the state of the company. These people will often engage with the CEO via a comment on the CEO blog, resulting in an online conversation that is as effective as, and probably more widely read than, a traditional, structured interview for print.

Public Relations

Companies that employ creative social media are often covered in a positive way in the mainstream media. *Fortune*, *Forbes*, the *Wall Street Journal*, the *New York Times*, and many of the most widely read publications in the U.S. and overseas are keen to cover the latest corporate social media trends, providing a ready vehicle for a company to be painted in a very positive light for its creativity and progressiveness.

For example, Comcast received a fair amount of coverage for its "Comcast Cares" program on Twitter, including a feature by Brian Stelter in the *New York Times* titled "Griping Online? Comcast Hears and Talks Back."

According to Stelter,

> "Comcast says the online outreach is part of a larger effort to revamp its customer service. In just about five months, Mr. Eliason, whose job redefines customer service, has reached out to well over 1,000 customers online."

Lyza Gardner, a Comcast customer interviewed for the piece, said she started off "very angry at Comcast," but was almost immediately placated when the company responded. "It's one thing to spit vitriol about a company when they can't hear you," she told the paper, but added "I immediately backed down and softened my tone when I knew I was talking to a real person."

Comcast, plagued by customer service issues, solved so many problems with this simple initiative. They took positive steps to improve customer service. They opened up the lines of communications and said "can we help?" They engaged openly with customers and provided more than marketing platitudes. They offered real help in the form of technical advice, contact information, and actual customer support. And they got great coverage for it.

All this took place under the watchful eyes of Twitter's three million users and ended up in first-tier coverage. In an age where mainstream media is devoting less editorial focus to technology and products and more to lifestyles and trends, this kind of positive coverage is invaluable.

The Tools

Now that we've talked about the strategy behind measuring social media, let's take a look at some of the many tools available that can help communicators gauge the success of their social media initiatives. These will provide insights into both quantitative and qualitative measures.

Web Analytics

As previously mentioned, web analytics provide many of the basic on-site measures of the success of your social media initiatives. These tools start with the free and inexpensive and can include some highly sophisticated and fairly expensive enterprise-grade applications.

One of the keys to the success of all of your social media efforts will be a congenial working relationship with your information technology organization. Looking beyond measurement, most of the decisions as to what tools and applications you will be able to use will be heavily influenced by your current IT environment, your company's technological capabilities, and even the priorities within your IT organization. It's important not to get into an adversarial relationship with IT. A good communicator understands at least some of the technological requirements behind the programs that he or she is trying to implement. You need to know enough to be dangerous.

In the area of measurement, for example, nearly every web analytics solution requires access to the company's internal IT infrastructure. In some cases the company may already have sophisticated web analytics tools in place. If you have additional requirements, you'll need to engage your IT people in discussions regarding your planned implementations and their ability to integrate those with the company's current infrastructure and analytics capabilities.

For the purposes of this discussion, we will interchangeably use the word *site* to mean any online social media vehicle that you are trying to assess. Each of the tools discussed may require modification to your blog, community, website home page, and so on. Typically, but not always, they will require the insertion of JavaScript code into each page. This is generally not difficult, but it will require the services of a web or blog developer. With the higher-end applications, this should be included in the systems integration offered by the vendor.

Google Analytics

Google Analytics is a simple yet very powerful tool for gathering and visualizing detailed web analytics. Google Analytics is extremely popular and is a formidable competitor to paid analytics tools. Naturally Google has a vested interest in letting companies assess their site performance, as many of the numbers generated through analytics are used to document the performance of Google's paid advertising programs.

Google Analytics will tell you how many unique visitors came to your site, which links they clicked to get there, how long they stayed on the site, and even which web browsers they are using and what parts of the world they are in. In addition to providing useful measures of overall traffic, this kind of detail can tell you which content is the most effective in driving traffic.

Enterprise-Grade Social Media Measurement

The following list covers some of the companies involved in social media measurement software and services. Most of these employ an extended approach that goes well beyond the site-based approach of web analytics. For example, these solutions in many cases can gather and analyze external links to the company's blogs and other social media sites. Each offers a varying degree of automation and user customizability. It is not practical in the short space of this book to analyze all the available tools, nor to make specific recommendations. This list is provided as a reference, and you should investigate each vendor thoroughly to determine whether its offering fits your budget, IT environment, and most importantly, whether it will help you gather the information you wish to collect.

This list is by no means all-inclusive, and you should also consult with your corporate web and IT organizations for their insights before making a selection in this area. The short paragraphs on each company are taken directly from the company websites. (I accept no responsibility for any hype found in these.)

- Radian6 (www.radian6.com)
  "Radian6 is focused on building the complete monitoring and analysis solution for PR and advertising professionals so they can be the experts in social media."

- Umbria (www.umbrialistens.com)
  "Umbria is a marketing intelligence company that analyzes social media—including blogs, message boards, Usenet, and product review sites. Umbria delivers not just data, but insights into brands, markets, consumers, and trends."

- BuzzLogic (www.buzzlogic.com)
  "With a growing suite of tools for bloggers and advertisers, as well as an ad network designed for today's conversational media landscape, Buzz-Logic offers all players in the media ecosystem insights and solutions for building a prosperous presence in social media."

- Visible Technologies (www.visibletechnologies.com)
  "Visible Technologies is a leading provider of online brand management solutions for companies and individuals in today's rapidly changing new media environment."

Blog Search

Blog search is another useful tool for finding out what companies are saying about your company out in the blogosphere. These specialized search engines will find many blogs that are invisible to conventional search engines. The two most popular of these are Technorati and Google Blog Search. One of the advantages of Google Blog Search is Google's handy alerts mechanism, which can provide you with real-time email alerts any time a new blog post or other web posting is published in which a particular term, such as your company name or your competitor's name, is used.

In addition to helping you find blog posts relevant to your company, Technorati will also tell you the ranking of the blog in which the post was made, which can help you "weight" rankings based on the "authority" (readership and prominence) of each blog. Technorati ranks each blog based on the number of other blogs linking to that blog and a number of other factors.

Blog Ranking

As previously mentioned, Technorati can give you interesting insight into the authority—the online prominence—of your company's social media sites as well as those of competitors, and those of people posting comments relevant to your company.

Another popular blog ranking service is Alexa (**Figure 7.1**), which lets users see free rankings for the top 500 global sites and the top 100 sites by country. Extended ranking data is available for purchase. Alexa offers a cool graphing tool to compare to several sites in a single view:

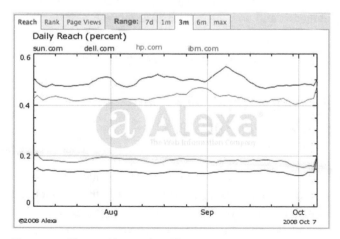

Figure 7.1 *Blog ranking service: Alexa*

Social Bookmarking

Many of the popular social bookmarking sites like Digg and deli.cio.us can also give you insight into the effectiveness of your social media programs. On Digg, you can see the number of times articles about your company, whether published by you or externally, have been selected by Digg users and how many "yes" and "no" votes have been cast in connection with each article. Similarly, bookmarks on deli.cio.us will tell you the number of users who have flagged as interesting information found online about your company.

Social Networks

Some measures of the effectiveness of your social network–based initiatives are easily found within the confines of the network itself. For example, on Facebook you can see the number of members of a company group or fans of the company page, as well as the number of comments. Similar measures are visible on MySpace and other social networks. Some of the more sophisticated enterprise-grade tools previously mentioned may be able to help you measure social network program effectiveness, and this is something you should consider in selecting a vendor.

Another Perspective

There are many approaches to measuring the effectiveness of social media programs. I've talked about a few, including both quantitative and qualitative measures, and those that are both easily found and nearly impossible to document. To gain some additional perspective, I asked Katie Delahaye Paine, a recognized authority on social media measurement, to provide her thoughts on the value of social media, and how it can be measured.

ESSAY: HOW TO MEASURE NAKED CONVERSATIONS

By Katie Delahaye Paine, CEO, KDPaine & Partners

Just mention the words *blog* and *measurement* in the same sentence and most people get that "deer in the headlights" look. Relax, this article isn't about measuring blogs, it's about measuring social media. There, isn't that better? No? Well read on... it really does get better, and easier.

First of all, we call it social media, because today "media" includes blogs as well as other forms of consumer generated two-way conversations, including everything from Facebook, MySpace, Flickr, and YouTube to Utterli, Twitter, and Second Life.

To understand how to measure social media, one first must understand that most of the rules of communications have changed. In the old days, whoever screamed loudest won. Communications was about reaching as many eyeballs or ears as possible for the least cost. Hence the emphasis on metrics like Ad Value Equivalency, which were purported to prove how cost-effective PR was in comparison to advertising. This also contributed to the total overload of communications, with the average individual seeing some 6,000 messages per day.

Then along came Google and search and the ability for users to create content, and the tectonic plates shifted. Now, to quote David Weinberger, author of *The Cluetrain Manifesto*, "there is no longer a market for your message." The vast majority of eyeballs and ears really don't care about your message. They are going online and searching for what interests them, forming networks with people of similar interests, and ignoring more and more of the mass communications that organizations are throwing at them.

So now success is less about how many eyeballs you have reached, and more about whether you are there when the right eyeballs go looking for you. Forget reach and frequency. Success in today's reality is measured not on how broad your reach is, but on how broad and deep your network is and what people actually do with the information you're putting out there. To put it in research terms, it is no longer about measuring outputs, but measuring outcomes. What this means is that it we now need to measure relationships and actions rather than eyeballs and column inches. And the good news is that as a result, measuring ROI may actually be easier.

In the olden days, way back in the twentieth century, it was all about how broad a net you could cast, how many people you reached, and how loudly you could scream. Today, with advanced web-analytic tools you can measure not just actions, but engagement. Networking sites like Facebook, MySpace, and Second Life, and services like Twitter and Utterli and LinkedIn bring the whole new dimension of engagement into the mix.

For these types of social media, what matters is how many connections or "friends" you have and how engaged these friends are with your brand or what you have to say. Without friends or followers nothing you do or say matters. And if those friends aren't commenting, voting for you or "favoriting" you, you really have no idea whether anyone is engaging in your brand.

While some might argue that you want to have "the right" friends (not just any) we're a long way from defining or measuring the value of specific friends in a network. What we can measure is the degree to which people comment, vote, or otherwise participate in what you're putting out there, *and* whether your social media activity is having an impact on web traffic, requests for information, or other outcomes.

Another key difference with this whole new world of social media is that everything is so transparent. You can look up Barack Obama or Sarah Palin on Facebook and see exactly how many friends (and enemies) they have. You can log on to Second Life and see exactly how many people are online at that very moment. All this transparency takes a lot of the mystery out of measurement. Instead of black boxes and bespoke algorithms, you can just go online and find a ranking, or the number of people in a network, or the extent of your links.

What is hardest for PR people to grasp is not the transparency, but the lack of control. The normal maxim for measurement is, "If you can't measure it, you can't manage it." The problem with measuring blogs is not how to do it, but rather that the nature of blogs renders management impossible. You simply can't *manage* what 10 million independent-minded, opinionated people are going to say. And woe to those who try, since the blogosphere resembles nothing more than a cornered porcupine that will automatically begin to throw darts the moment it sees someone trying to control it.

The following pages provide some guidelines, as well as tips, tools and techniques that can be used to get a handle on this easily measured but hard to manage phenomenon.

WHAT ARE YOU MEASURING?

The first thing to remember is that in addition to being irrelevant, *reach* in the blogosphere is essentially not possible. For those obsessed with old media metrics, there are no equivalent numbers like *audited circulation* figures for blogs at the time of this writing. The Interactive Advertising Bureau recently challenged the two leading eyeball owners, Nielsen and comScore, to come up with an accurate system of measuring online viewership and found that they were off by 35 million eyeballs—roughly the population of Texas and hardly a rounding error. Most influential blogs don't even accept advertising and therefore have no reason to publish impression or circulation figures. So there is simply no way to compare the "reach" of a *New York Times* placement with a mention in Shel Israel's Global Neighbourhoods blog, unless you know Shel well enough to ask him how many readers he has—something that simply isn't feasible when there are 80 million blogs out there.

So what should you be measuring? The simple answer is: "whatever it is that you want the audience to do." Do you want them to request more information? Get more engaged with your brand? Make a contribution? Vote? Buy something? Then that's what you should be measuring.

The second element in this very large discussion about measuring blogs and other consumer-generated media (CGM) is to get clear about what elements of a social media program you're trying to measure.

When people ask "how do you measure social media?" they may be talking about measuring the value of their own corporate or internal blog, or they may be talking about how to measure the impact of Facebook pages on their reputation or their sales.

OPTION #1: BLOG VALUE EQUIVALENCY—MEASURING YOUR OWN CORPORATE OR INTERNAL BLOG

This measurement assumes that you're a blogger or you're running a corporate blog, and you want to calculate the ROI of that blog. There are several ways to calculate the value. If you are concerned with the value of your corporate blog, you can calculate the value the same way you would a house—by looking at the comparable value for which other similar blogs have sold. There's a nifty little applet at www.business-opportunities.biz/projects/how-much-is-your-blog-worth that will tell you the absolute value of your blog based on your traffic, your links, and what other blogs have sold for recently. Alternatively, you can calculate the engagement factor of your blog by looking at the number of visits plus the number of links, comments, repeat visitors, registrations, and trackbacks for your blog.

Another such metric is the Conversation Index, which refers to the ratio between the number of posts the author creates and the number of comments and trackbacks the blog receives. The theory is that the degree to which you are generating conversation is an indicator of the value of the blog. So, if in any given month you add 50 posts to your blog and you get 100 comments on those 50 posts, your Conversation Index is 2:1. The downside of this metric is that there's no way we can calculate similar ratios for your competition, so there's no way to benchmark your results.

For some organizations, measurement is as simple as adding a unique URL to a blog posting and tracking the number of sales or leads it generates. Elisa

Camahort of BlogHer fame starts blogs for her clients in the theater business, getting actors to post their thoughts about the show and the town. By tracking click-throughs, the number of people who first visit the blog and then click on a link to the ticket sales site, she was able to measure thousands of dollars in ticket revenue originating from the blog.

OPTION #2: MEASURING THE INFLUENCE OF THE BLOGS IN WHICH YOU ARE MENTIONED

This measurement is the social media equivalent to weighting publications or reporters based on their circulation figures or reach. Since there isn't a social media equivalent of reach, there are several other ways that organizations are determining the impact of the blogs in which their brands are discussed.

One way of deciding which blogs are important is to consider Web Rank: Web Rank is the rank of the site in numerical order, of all Internet sites worldwide, based on a sample of millions of web users who have voluntarily installed a special measurement toolbar in their web browsers. Compete is one such service. It provides a toolbar to users, and this toolbar aggregates data on sites visited while users browse the web. Web Rank takes into account both the number of visitors to a site and the average number of page views by each visitor while browsing the site. Web Rank is based on three months of aggregated traffic data and is updated monthly. The measurement system includes the rank of web-based forums, message boards, and discussion groups, but it does not measure the rank of clips from Usenet newsgroups.

There's a site called www.xenureturns.com that lists a variety of rankings. Just type in the URL of the blog and you'll get a sense of how important it is. Since a new blog is created every second of every day (according to the latest State of the Blogosphere report by Technorati), one needs to carefully evaluate the claims of the various monitoring services. There are free services such as Technorati, Sphere, and Ice Rocket that offer robust search engines that can call up all blogs that mention your brand. Alternatively, there are paid services such as CyberAlert, CustomScoop, Moreover, and e-Watch that automatically deliver blog postings to your desktop. What you choose depends upon the reach you desire. As of this writing, Technorati monitors more than 70 million, Feedster monitors 80 million, and CyberAlert and CustomScoop each claim 6+ million blogs. Nielsen BuzzMetrics boasts a population of more than 25 million blogs.

Market Sentinel has established a system to measure blog authority, based on the number of times a particular blog shows up in a discussion of your specific brand. Their methodology is explained in their paper "Measuring the Influence of Blogs on Corporate Reputation," which is available on their website www.marketsentinel.com.

OPTION #3: MEASURING THE IMPACT OF EXTERNAL SOCIAL MEDIA ON YOUR BUSINESS

Again, the key to measuring the impact of external social media on your business is having good web analytics. Even a simple free program like Google Analytics will tell you the origin of most of the traffic to your website, making it relatively easy to determine how effective Twitter is versus Facebook or Google in generating traffic to your website.

OPTION#4: MEASURING THE IMPACT OF EXTERNAL SOCIAL MEDIA ON YOUR REPUTATION

The most common form of blog measurement has to do with gaining a better understanding of the impact blogs have on reputation. Using technology such as natural language processing (NLP) and heuristics, you can scan large volumes of postings to determine the content, tonality, and sentiment of your coverage. People are concerned that a potential disaster (for example, Dell Hell) can erupt and spook customers and/or Wall Street. So they make sure that every mention of their brand is tracked and that any hint of a problem is reported. They also use this kind of measurement to listen to customers and find out what is on their minds.

Do you have to slog through 1,000 postings a month? Not necessarily. What you measure and how you measure it depends on several factors. First of all, how frequently does your brand (or the competition) appear and how important are the blogs in which it does appear to your audience? You only want to read postings from the blogs and sites that really matter to your target audiences. So frequently the first step is to ask your target audience what is important to them. The next step is figuring out exactly what people are saying about you. As it happens, any conversation taking place, be it in your living room, on Twitter, Facebook, or in Second Life falls into one of 27 basic categories:

- Acknowledging receipt of information
- Advertising something
- Answering a question
- Asking a question
- Augmenting a previous post
- Calling for action
- Disclosing personal information
- Distributing media
- Expressing agreement

- Expressing criticism
- Expressing support
- Expressing surprise
- Giving a heads-up
- Giving a shout-out
- Making a joke
- Making a suggestion
- Making an observation
- Offering a greeting
- Offering an opinion
- Putting out a wanted ad
- Rallying support
- Recruiting people
- Responding to criticism
- Showing dismay
- Soliciting comments
- Soliciting help
- Starting a poll

Any video that is produced falls into one of the following categories:

- Advertisement
- Animation
- Demonstration
- Event/performance
- Fiction
- Film
- Home video
- Instructional video
- Interview
- Lecture
- Montage
- Music video
- News broadcast
- Promotional video
- Sightseeing/tour
- Slideshow
- Speech
- Television show
- Video log

Using these categories enables you to compare and contrast your reputation in different types of social media. After you've determined the nature of the conversation, the next step is figuring out what is being said.

In the media and in most newsgroups, the vast majority of what is said about a particular organization is neutral. But the unfettered and unfiltered nature of the blogosphere brings more opinions, and frequently more negative opinions. Remember to step back as far as you can and remain objective. Think like your target audience. Just because someone leaked a piece of information or got a name wrong is no reason to respond or get involved in a discussion. We recommend tracking the following criteria:

- **Sentiment:** What was the tone of the conversation? Did it portray your brand in a positive or negative light? If the tone of the posting leaves a reader less likely to do business with your organization, then it is negative. If the posting leaves a reader more likely to do business with your organization, or it recommends the brand, then it is positive. If it essentially just discusses facts, then it is neutral or balanced.

- **Dominance/visibility:** How deeply does the posting discuss the brand? Is it just a passing mention or does the blogger go into the subject in depth with numerous links?

- **Type of interaction:** What was the nature of the interaction? Was the posting designed to solve a problem, compare different brands, or simply to allow the author to rant?

- **Nature of discussion:** What was the nature of the discussion? Was it a true dialog with an extensive exchange of ideas, or was it just bantering back and forth?

- **Messaging:** Did it contain one or more of your key messages?

- **Positioning:** Does it position your brand the way you'd like to be known or in some other, less desirable way?

- **Optimal content score:** In essence this is a score based on what you decide is the "perfect mention" in social media. Perhaps it is one that prominently mentions the brand in a favorable light compared to the competition. Or perhaps the "optimal content" is being left out of a conversation altogether. Either way with the optimal content score, you alone determine what the desirable outcome is.

Why Do I Need to Bother Measuring Social Media at All?

If you don't want to start a conversation with your marketplace or hear what your customers are saying about you, feel free to ignore social media altogether. You probably won't be in business for very much longer, but at least you won't have had to deal with this whole new realm of communications.

However, you also should be aware that most journalists today rely on blogs for story ideas, to check facts, and to track down and investigate scandals and rumors. So if you care about what key journalists are saying about you, you should probably be measuring social media.

If you are still up in the air about whether or not blogs are important for you, conduct a quick poll of your audience and find out just how influential the blogosphere is. There's lots of generic research out there, but most organizations would be better off surveying their own customers to find out just how big of an impact CGM and the blogosphere has. Or just use Sphere or Technorati to find out if anyone is blogging about you.

How Will Blogs Ultimately Impact Your Organizational Goals?

Do customer complaints on blogs pose a threat to your reputation? Your sales? Is one of your goals to get a particular point of view or position across? Do you need to influence a particular analyst? If there is definitely no clear tie between your organization's goals and the blogosphere, then exit out of this article immediately and go learn about measuring more relevant media. (As in any communications activity, if it doesn't support a specific corporate goal, why are you doing it?)

On the other hand, if developing a network of influencers around your product, your idea, or your service is important, then a blog will be a very useful tool. Once you've answered these questions, you can move on to deciding how and what you want to measure.

Some Closing Thoughts

Ultimately, Katie and I are in complete agreement that social media measurement isn't the same as traditional media measurement, that there are many methods available to communicators, and that you need to set your own goals and expectations and then measure them. Yes, social media has value. Yes, it can be measured, but it's often difficult to measure. But that doesn't mean companies shouldn't do everything possible to make these measurements. There are dozens of approaches to assessing and measuring the value of social media, and the right approach will vary based on your goals and expectations, your budget, the capabilities within your company, and many other factors.

Some closing thoughts on developing a successful measurement strategy:

- Build numeric goals and the tools to measure them into your social media initiatives.

- Have realistic expectations. Revenue is hard to measure in any communications program.

- However remotely, tie social media measurement strategy back to business and communications strategy and objectives.

- Be nice to your company's web and IT folks. They can make or break your social media programs.

- Learn about all the tools available to you and use the ones that give you the most useful information. Learn how to interpret that information to apply it as a measure of success.

What is certain is that we are well beyond asking the question, "Is social media a fad, or can companies use it to create real business value?" Yes, social media is creating business value. And the methods for measuring that value are improving every day.

SocialCorp 2.0: Corporate Communications Inside Out

Having read this far in the book, maybe having become involved in a couple of social media programs, and done some research, you've probably come to a pretty good understanding of the state of social media in corporate communications.

But just when you thought it was safe to go back in the water, things have started shifting again. The world of social media is a fast-moving one. You may be well along your way to being completely current with everything going on in social media, but the key to being competitive is not to be current but to be ahead of the game.

This chapter takes a brief look at some of the changes going on in social media, and communications in general, that you should start thinking about now.

The latest tools and trends, the hot new applications, sites, and services, the stuff everyone is talking about but which doesn't yet make complete sense, are all indicators of how people like to communicate now and how their preferences are shifting. As a corporate communicator, you'll want to look out a couple of years to see what new technology and new applications might help you best reach your audiences as their habits change.

In some cases, in areas like customer service, things have literally turned inside out. In other cases, it's a metaphor for the radical changes happening to things like what a brand is, who owns it, who controls the message, and where the important conversations are taking place.

The impact of some of these will make immediate sense in a corporate environment, others may seem a little obscure, and still others may make you laugh.

Five Changes in the State of Social Media

This section identifies five "current states," five things about social media that are fairly well established today, and then a future state for each, signaled by trends in social media applications, user preferences, and communications strategies. There are of course many other changes going on, but this framework is useful for thinking about a great many of the changes that will affect you in the next year or so:

- Speed→Brevity

- Participation→Chaos

- Letting Go→Taking Back

- Engagement→Doing Business

- Wild Wild West→The Civilized World

Speed→Brevity

The first shift taking place is from speed to brevity. It's pretty well established that social media is "fast" in a number of ways. Consider for example how long it takes to post a news item with links and images on a conventional static website versus the amount of time required to do the same thing on a blog or social media newsroom.

Consider also how quickly news and other information are broadcast via RSS the moment they're published. Even social bookmarking tools like Digg and Delicious let you share items with potentially thousands of people with just a few clicks of the mouse.

What's going to matter next is not speed but brevity. Attention spans seem to be getting shorter and shorter, and at the same time, trends in online content are adapting to this fact. The emergence of microblogging, with its super short, text-only updates, is testimony to this.

Maybe brevity isn't the word, maybe it's *conciseness*. Or both. The point is messages are going to get physically shorter in length, and smaller in size, whether those messages are sent in text, audio, or video form.

We will soon see the online equivalent of the proverbial Lord's Prayer on the head of a pin.

Here's an example of the relentlessness of the drive to make things more concise. This URL from HP Shopping is 209 characters long:

http://www.shopping.hp.com/webapp/shopping/series_can.do;HHOJSID= JnYPJCpcvQMNGRylrDlCyVXhyzLLlQHrMo1lHLPvnWGTT6hKxYW1! 521570135?storeName=computer_store&landing=notebooks&a1= Category&v1=Versatile%20performance

It won't fit in a 140-character Twitter update. Try memorizing it. Try emailing it, and it might break up and become unusable. Try sending it from an iPhone, which (as of the publication of this book) has no copy and paste capability.

Tinyurl.com is a website that allows users to reduce URLs for exactly these reasons, and because long URLs are ugly. Tinyurl creates a shorter URL that refers the user to the original URL. If we run the HP URL through Tinyurl, here's how it comes out:

http://tinyurl.com/5ot5dy

It's now just 25 characters long, but wait, there's more. No, there's less! The same URL rendered by is.gd, a more recent entry in URL shortening, is:

http://is.gd/4KcQ

Now it's 17 characters. A few characters never mattered before, but now that updates might be limited to 140 characters, or people might be sending links from their phones where they are sometimes charged by the character, it makes a big difference.

People aren't just cramming more information into smaller spaces for efficiency. People have short attention spans, particularly online. Nick Carr, in a piece titled "Is Google Making Us Stupid?" in *The Atlantic*, July/August 2008, writes:

> "...what the Net seems to be doing is chipping away my capacity for concentration and contemplation. My mind now expects to take in information the way the Net distributes it: in a swiftly moving stream of particles."

This new way of "taking in" information manifests itself in many ways.

Quincy Smith, President of CBS Interactive, speaking in November 2007 at NewTeeVee Live (an Internet video conference), said that 70 percent of all online video viewing is in clip form (short segments) and not full episodes. The preferred length is around three minutes, not coincidentally, about that of the typical rock video.

How long are the information pieces your corporate communications team produces? People aren't going to stop reading long written pieces and watching long video altogether, but if there are more than 250 words or more than a couple of minutes of audio or video, people might skip right over them.

Following Twitter's lead, services in both the microblogging space and elsewhere have introduced foreshortened content strategies into their offerings.

Blippr, for example, offers user-generated reviews of books, games, music, and movies, in 160 characters or less. (Better bookmark is.gd for later use!)

And Yammer, winner of the best of show award at the 2008 TechCrunch50 event, brings Twitter-like brief status updates inside the corporate firewall. Yammer describes itself as "a tool for making companies and organizations more productive through the exchange of short frequent answers to one simple question: 'What are you working on?'" According to TechCrunch, "There is such a huge demand for this type of service that 10,000 people and 2,000 organizations signed up for the service the first day it launched."

Other examples of the shrinking social media content footprint abound. There's 12seconds.tv, which lets users record, you guessed it, 12-second videos, the idea being that 12 seconds of video is analogous to 140 characters of text. The verdict is still out on that one.

Participation→Chaos

One possible name for the current time in the history of social media and communications in general might be *The Participation Era*. Many large companies are using social media to create situations in which consumers can actively participate in the management of the company. We see this in the executive blog, where in some cases a consumer can chat one-on-one with the company's CEO about strategy, new products, and new markets. The concept of the customer forum is a popular one, with dozens of successful examples.

But just as the last wave of social media helped companies participate in these conversations, the latest wave of applications has unleashed millions of online consumer conversations that the company might be completely unaware of.

These conversations have risks and opportunities. Somewhere out there, people are saying great stuff about your company and you don't know about it. And somewhere else, people are trashing your company and you can't respond.

Third-party sites like Get Satisfaction allow users to ask companies questions and, provided the company has a registered account, get a response from one of their representatives. Since it's a third-party site, consumers seem to be more willing to trust its outcomes. And increasingly, users frustrated by a company's own complex, web-based customer support forums and poorly staffed, proprietary "live chat" support are flocking to social media, the preferred channel for all communications of compliments and complaints about the companies they do business with.

Adobe is one of many companies responding to customer inquiries on Get Satisfaction:

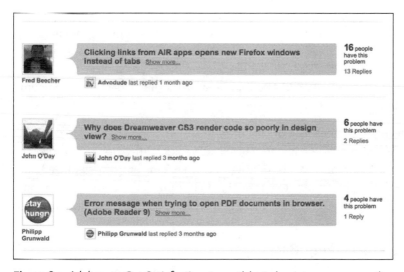

Figure 8.1 *Adobe uses* Get Satisfaction *to participate in customer conversations.*

Consumers also use social bookmarking sites like Reddit, Digg, Propeller, and StumbleUpon, to "vote" and comment on items. When Apple Computer, Inc. announced the new iPhone, for example, there were hundreds of items posted on each of these sites, with consumers passionately weighing in with their reactions.

Here, an article about a new Seagate hard disk drive has received 869 "Diggs" and 179 comments. That's an awful lot of interesting conversation!

Figure 8.2 *Diggs about a new Seagate disk drive.*

In a way, these sites also put search engine optimization, (techniques to improve the placement of search results), once the domain of the corporate website operator, into the hand of users, as they use their votes to push items to the top of the "page," making them more visible to other users.

User commentary builds buzz around a particular story, regardless of the relevance or importance of the original story. A site like Fark actually pokes fun at news stories and cultural disasters by adding their own commentary to news headlines. Newcomers Mixx and Plime raise the bar by categorizing news stories and offering Diggs for photos and videos, as well. And in keeping with the "green" trend, C2NN, EarthFrisk, and Hugg are building communities by sharing earth-friendly news.

With the rapid proliferation of new third-party services dedicated to customer support, and the popularity of social bookmarking sites as forums for consumer discussions, we are shifting from an era of company-managed participatory communications to one of chaotic, unpredictable communications that will be increasingly difficult for companies to monitor and participate in.

Letting Go→Taking Back

Companies responding to a perceived loss of control brought on by social media are doing so in a variety of ways. Some are panicking and using "old school" strategies, while others have figured out how to "turn communications inside out" and use new media and new communications habits to their advantage.

Inside companies, people are clearly confused about social media. According to a September 2008 survey by Coleman Parkes Research, "more than 75 percent of companies worldwide admit that social networking will come into the business by stealth if not proactively managed," yet only 18 percent have any kind of strategy for using these technologies with employees.

One of the worst responses to the rising popularity of social networks is to use information technology (IT), a company's computer hardware, software, and network, to physically block social networking sites. A 2007 report by Internet security company Barracuda Networks indicated that slightly more than half of its customers used the company's products to block employee access to MySpace, Facebook, or both. It's unfortunate that companies are turning to security technology vendors to solve what should be dealt with as a policy issue. And while some employees most certainly abuse company Internet usage policies, the vast majority are responsible and ethical and cannot help but see the company as "Big Brother" for taking such draconian steps to deal with the social networking "problem."

Other, more open-minded companies realize employees have preferred methods of communications, and the best way to engage them as partners in the success of the business is to adapt, not prohibit, these new tools.

As mentioned earlier in the book, companies are responding to the boom in social networking by developing internal clones of popular social networks and social media tools. By doing so, they bring their employees the kind of communications experience they enjoy most and that will make them the most productive.

Others are extending the prevailing metaphors to make more powerful use of social media.

Dell's IdeaStorm is an example of this. IdeaStorm is effective because it's more than a customer forum. It's a full-blown customer engagement program and a catalyst for change in the company's products and services. Not only do customers post ideas, Dell chooses the best of these for implementation and reports on its progress. As of September 2008, 10,000 ideas had been posted and 200 had been implemented. By consumer vote, the most popular suggestion was that the company offer the Linux operating system pre-installed on its computers, a service Dell introduced in August 2008.

Another example of communications turned inside out is Best Buy's Blue Shirt Nation (BSN), a company-sponsored social network for employees.

BSN is the antithesis of the company intranet site. It exists "outside the firewall," (on the public Internet), where it can be accessed by any employee. Instead of using IT to block access to the site, employees are urged to spend time there engaging with "a robust community of people with a common interest, Best Buy. They share knowledge, best practices, frustrations, aspirations, and jokes." So wrote Best Buy's Gary Koelling on his personal blog.

Participation on BSN is optional and driven by word of mouth and referrals. Within a year of BSN's launch, 20,000 of Best Buy's employees had signed up.

According to Koelling, BSN members have "impacted huge changes to Best Buy. Like the 401(k) Challenge—a video contest hosted on BSN to promote enrollment in our 401(k)...(which) resulted in a 30 percent increase in 401(k) enrollments. That's 40,000 employees signing up for the 401(k) that hadn't before."

Engagement→Doing Business

Another shift is from engagement and other "soft" measures of social media value to harder, in more ways than one, business measures. It's widely recognized that measuring the effectiveness of any online communications initiative is not easy. Measuring the amount of revenue created by a blog or online community is almost impossible.

Some proposed new measures of social media effectiveness, like return on engagement and return on influence, may prove useful, but others are merely smokescreens for the bigger issue of trying to assess measurable business value from social media initiatives.

Engagement is valuable, make no mistake. But no CFO ever said "we need 15 percent more engagement next quarter."

As Chapter 7, "Can You Count Everything that Counts?," suggests, there are numerous enterprise-grade tools available to help companies monitor social media effectiveness. Traditional web metrics, like page views, downloads of software, and the number of times a video was launched, are useful, too.

But 2008 ushered in one of the worst economic climates in world history. Return on investment has always been important in large companies, and particularly in publicly held companies, but a focus on bottom-line results will sharpen over the next few years.

Companies will need to respond in a couple of different ways. Where possible, we will see more integration between the company's social media sites, such as blogs and communities, and it's "back-end" systems, in areas like order entry, customer relationship management (CRM), and so on.

SalesForce, the leading online CRM company, now offers IdeaExchange, which helps customer communities like Dell's IdeaStorm and Starbucks' My Starbucks Idea integrate (share data) with the respective company's CRM.

Relative newcomer InsideView, which offers what it calls "business search and intelligence," refers to the convergence of social media with CRM and other enterprise applications as a "socialprise...the junction of traditional enterprise applications and social networks."

Also, as freewheeling sites like Twitter move to advertising revenue–driven models, companies will be better able to measure their social media initiatives on these sites.

This can backfire, though. Clive Thompson reported in the November 2008 *Wired* magazine that after CNET launched a redesign of its social network UrbanBaby, which it purchased in 2006, "all hell broke loose." CNET changed the way posts appeared on the site's home page and added a wide sidebar to accommodate advertising. Users rebelled and asked CNET to restore the site's user experience, and when CNET did not, writes Thompson, "a couple of work-at-home computer programmers—longtime UrbanBaby users themselves—launched a rival site called YouBeMom, which he says now hosts more traffic than UrbanBaby while improving on its original user experience.

This unfortunately is the paradox of social media. As various sites change their look and feel over time, specifically as they become more commercial and focus more attention on enabling advertising and capturing and sharing specific user data, users often rebel, migrating to some other site that they see as less commercial and less invasive.

Wild Wild West→The Civilized World

The final area in which there are big changes ahead is in the regulation of social media. In Chapter 6, "Balancing Social Media Risk and Reward," we looked at the state of social media ethics and law, and some of the high-profile social media ethical gaffes committed by, sadly, some of the world's largest and most trusted companies.

There, someone once wrote, lies the rub. New media does not need new morality. The so-called "wild wild west" claim (the rules are being written as we speak, uncharted territory, blah blah blah) in defense of ethical missteps never held up, but it will be less and less palatable in the next 12 to 18 months as regulators step in and tighten control over anti-social social media behavior.

Not all regulation is bad. But some will be. If Tim Couch's HB 775 is enacted, though that seems unlikely today, anyone leaving a comment on any public blog or customer community must register and expose his or her full name and other information in order to participate. This would be great news for companies that want to more closely track participation in their social media initiatives, but it would mean death for spontaneous, open conversation.

There are sure to be many additional bills proposed, and eventually enacted, that will affect corporate social media activities.

Other laws will affect the behavior of both companies and consumers on social networks (and everywhere online). According to Halt Abuse, "there are 45 cyberstalking (and related) laws on the books." A specific federal law, Federal CyberStalking Bill S2991 is on hold.

In 2006, H.R. 3402, the "Violence Against Women and Department of Justice Reauthorization Act of 2005" was signed into law, essentially defining and criminalizing some forms of online harassment. It states in part that whoever uses "any device or software that can be used to originate telecommunications or other types of communications that are transmitted, in whole or in part, by the Internet... without disclosing his identity and with intent to annoy, abuse, threaten, or harass any person...who receives the communications...shall be fined under title 18 or imprisoned not more than two years, or both." Strangely, this piece of legislation seems to permit the behavior if the user identifies himself/herself.

In addition to stepped-up regulation, we will no doubt see efforts made by social networks and other sites to improve their Terms of Service (TOS) and enforcement thereof. This is exactly what happened in online chat, as AOL and Yahoo in particular emerged from the almost anarchistic culture of the online "bulletin board," to that of the family-friendly web "destination."

The Future of Corporate Social Media

There you have it, in just over 3,000 words, the future of social media as it will affect corporate communications. There will be plenty of other things coming down the pike that will surprise all of us in the next couple of years. You'll see the trends mentioned here playing out soon, in a way that will directly affect your work.

SocialCorp 2.0: Start Now!

Keeping in mind not only these five major shifts, but everything covered in the book, here are some suggestions for getting your company ready to be a SocialCorp 2.0:

Be ethical. It's the right way, it's most likely the way your company wants to do business, and people who behave unethically, in addition to being rotten, will get caught, and the consequences will be substantial.

Be brief. People just don't have the attention spans they used to have. Make your point quickly and concisely. This is a good discipline for any corporate communicator.

Don't stay current, stay ahead. Changes in social media trends and technology affecting the corporate communicator are happening faster than ever. Blogging, for example, took nearly a decade after its introduction to find its way into anything like the mainstream. Meanwhile microblogging appeared from nowhere in 2006 and was in use by millions by 2007.

Maintain just enough control. One of the themes that runs throughout this book is the need to balance the transparent, conversational nature of social media with the obligations of a large corporation. You have to exercise some degree of control over the social media programs you oversee. This control could be over brand, message, or measurement, but there's not going to be much budget lying around to do social media just because it's cool.

Be willing to take some risks. Every new venture requires some risk-taking or it wouldn't be worth doing and it wouldn't rise above what the competition has to offer. The benefits of corporate social media are clear, and the risks are not that great if properly managed.

Hopefully, this book has provided you with the fundamentals to start your company down the path, or lead it into the next phase, of becoming a SocialCorp.

A primary objective of this book is to help you benefit from what others have learned along the way, inside and outside major corporations, as they adopt social media, sometimes with stunning success, other times not. But it is a fascinating phenomenon, still in its early days, and we all have a chance to keep learning, to share what we learn, and to use these new communications tools to change our companies, and the world, for the better.

Glossary

A

aggregator: An aggregator is a tool that allows users to subscribe to and display multiple RSS feeds in a convenient format. These can be desktop or web-based applications. Popular news aggregators (aka news readers) are NetVibes (www.netvibes.com), Bloglines (www.bloglines.com), and Google Blog Reader (www.google.com/reader).

AIR: Short for Adobe Integrated Runtime, AIR is a new Adobe software environment that allows a program to run on multiple operating systems and hardware, much in the way Java does. AIR allows applications to be installed on the local operating system and accessed from the desktop just like the other applications that the desktop user runs. At the same time, AIR applications can access online information. AIR applications can run either online or offline, but the environment is aimed at web developers. The eBay Desktop and Google Analytics are examples of prototypical AIR applications.

AJAX: Short for Asynchronous JavaScript and XML, it is a term that describes a new approach to using a number of existing technologies together, including the following: HTML or XHTML, Cascading Style Sheets, JavaScript, the Document Object Model, XML, XSLT, and the XMLHttpRequest object. When these technologies are combined in the AJAX model, web applications are able to make quick, incremental updates to the user interface without reloading the entire browser page. AJAX is often seen as the defining foundation of Web 2.0.

Akismet: A popular comment spam filter for WordPress blogs.

anonoblog: A blog site authored by a person or persons who don't publish their real name(s).

API: An acronym for Application Programming Interface. An API is the protocol by which a computer system or application allows *requests* to be made of it by other programs, allowing for data to be exchanged. APIs in Web 2.0 applications allow the data from these applications to be reused by other applications and services.

archives: Most often in the form of an index page, archives organize blog posts or entries by either category or date.

astroturfing: An attempt to falsify a grassroots consumer movement through deceptive means. The term originated in politics and was coined by Senator Lloyd Bentsen. In social media, astroturfing usually manifests itself when people post positive comments about a company on blogs and in online communities without revealing that they are employees and/or representatives of the company. In some cases, companies hire third parties, such as public relations agencies, to engage in astroturfing. Another form of astroturfing is the practice of hiring evangelists who chat favorably about a company on various social networks without revealing their affiliations. The European Union has outlawed the practice.

Atom: A popular feed format used for syndicating content.

autodiscovery: In RSS terminology, autodiscovery is the process used by web spiders to look for RSS content. When autodiscovery is enabled for your RSS feed, browsers and aggregators can then automatically detect it, making it easier for users to subscribe to your content.

avatar: A graphical image or likeness that is used to represent someone online. Many bloggers, forum members, and microbloggers use avatars. They are usually, but not always, thumbnail photographs of the account holder. In virtual reality worlds such as Second Life, an avatar is a three-dimensional animated representation of a person.

B

beta: A stage of product development. The term is usually applied to new software or social networking applications that are still in development. Applications and programs released in beta set expectations among the user base and encourage users to find and report problems to the developers to be resolved. Beta testing can be used to get user feedback and to develop early interest in a social media site or service.

blog: (n.) Short for web log, a blog is a web page that serves as a publicly accessible personal journal for an individual or a group of people. Sometimes updated daily, blogs often reflect the personality of the author. (v.) To author a web log. Other forms: blogger (a person who blogs).

blogola: The term comes from the radio term *payola*, which originated in the 1950s. In its original use, payola occurred when record company executives paid DJs to play certain songs and to "talk up" particular artists and records.

In the social media world, blogola typically describes a situation in which a blogger is given free merchandise, often with a request that the blogger review the product. Sometimes this request implies a favorable review in exchange for the free product.

Many bloggers have discontinued accepting free merchandise, choosing instead to return all review products to the manufacturer. In some areas this is more difficult than it sounds. For example, a reviewer cannot return food and wine.

blogosphere: The term is an expression used to describe the "world of blogs," or "all of the blogs in existence." Blogs, and their communities, authors, and readers, are all connected components of the blogosphere.

blogroll: A list of blogs that the blog's author likes and reads regularly. It generally appears on the sidebar of the blog. It is considered bad form to ask others to add you to their blogrolls.

bot: A piece of software that mimics human behavior in order to surreptitiously add content, like a post or comment, to a website. Bots are most often used for spamming.

brandjacking: A term used to describe a situation when a person or company "hijacks" the brand identity of another company. This could include the unauthorized use of the company name, logos, product photography, product names, and even website URLs. Several corporate accounts on Twitter, for example, have turned out to be bogus. This is one of the more blatant forms of brandjacking, in which an unauthorized person claims to be an official representative of the company.

Another milder form, which occurs often on Facebook, is the unauthorized use in an online discussion group or forum of the company's brand identity. In many cases, this occurs on fan pages and groups created by people who are enthusiastic about the company and its products. If the discussions in the group are largely favorable to the company, it may choose not to police this activity, but it could be a violation of copyright or trademark law.

C

captcha: A message requiring the user to retype a set of characters based on a graphic image into an onscreen form. The captcha tool is meant to ensure that the entity attempting to access a site, leave a comment, and so on, is a person and not a software program or spam bot.

chicklet (sometimes chiclet): A graphical feed button displayed on a blog or web page, usually a small rectangle, which when clicked, allows a user to subscribe to the feed from a blog, website, and so on.

comment: A response to something someone has posted on his or her blog. Comments are generally much shorter than posts.

comment spam: Any comment that has been posted to a blog solely for the purpose of generating an inbound or incoming link to the comment author's site or blog. Most often comment spam is irrelevant to the content of the blog it is posted on.

contributor: A writer who contributes to a web-based publication, such as a blog, community, forum, and so on. Some blogs, for example, have multiple authors or contributors who post and interact with a community of readers.

cookie: Information that your web browser keeps in memory about your activities at a particular site. Cookies track things like logins and passwords and other user information to make it easier to use a site when it is revisited after the initial visit.

Creative Commons license: A licensing concept created by Creative Commons that builds upon traditional copyright practices to define possibilities that exist between the standard "all rights reserved" full copyright and public domain "no rights reserved." A Creative Commons license lets you dictate how others may use your work. The Creative Commons license also allows you to keep your copyright while allowing others to copy and distribute your work provided they give you credit. For online work you can also select a license that generates "some rights reserved" or a "no rights reserved" statement for your published work.

D

dashboard: The administration area in a blog software program that allows the administrator to post content, check traffic, upload files, see who has linked to the blog, manage comments, and so on.

DataPortability: The DataPortability Working Group is an industry data portability standards working group that educates, designs, and advocates interoperable data portability to users, developers, and vendors. The Data-Portability Working Group defines data portability as "the option to share or move your personal data between trusted applications and vendors."

date-based archives: The archives of a blog site, organized by time-stamp. Almost every blog will have some form of time-stamp, and many archives are listed along the sidebar.

Delicious (or del.icio.us): A social bookmarking website that serves as a bookmarks manager for users, similar to a collection of favorite links. Users can add bookmarks to their Delicious lists, categorize the bookmarks, tag them, and also share them with others. On some blogs the words *del.icio.us* may appear below a blog post as a hyperlink that readers can click to submit the post to their Delicious bookmarks.

Digg: A community-based website where users submit content and rate that content by "Digging" or "voting up" the content they like. A submission that earns a larger number of Diggs, and therefore is more popular with users, is moved to the Digg homepage to the category of content it belongs in. The Digg website was founded by Kevin Rose and launched in November 2004.

domain name: The identifying name of an Internet site. The domain name of the author's site is www.socializedpr.com.

Dooced: A term meaning "getting fired for the content written in a blog post or website." From the popular site, Dooced (by an author who once vented about her company—and got fired because of what was written).

dynamic content: Website or blog content that changes frequently and engages the reader. Dynamic content can include animations, video, or audio. Also called rich content.

E

ecosystem: A community and its environment functioning as a whole. The blogosphere can be viewed as an ecosystem. Certain sites, like Twitter, have their own ecosystems of supporting sites and services that extend the functionality and usefulness of the main site.

editorial calendar: A long-term editorial plan, traditionally associated with print media but also applicable to online publications such as blogs. An editorial calendar defines themes and topics, by month and sometimes day, to be covered in the publication.

edublog: A blog focused on education.

EFF: The Electronic Frontier Foundation, founded in 1990, whose charter is to "confront cutting-edge issues defending free speech, privacy, innovation, and consumer rights today" in the digital world.

embed: To copy data or multimedia from one blog or website and paste it into another. Embedding is very common with videos and widgets. A typical use of embedding is the inclusion of a video "player," such as the YouTube player, in a blog or website.

entry: An individual post or article published on a blog. Each of these entries, while appearing in an index, are also web pages unto themselves.

event blog: A blog specifically launched as a companion to an event (such as a product launch or a conference)

F

feed aggregator: See *aggregator*.

FeedBlitz: An online service that captures the output of a blog or other site's RSS feed and converts it to email updates, making it easy for content owners, bloggers, and marketers to share updates to their web content with their readers via email.

FeedBurner: FeedBurner is a feed aggregator and subscription service that allows users to "burn" multiple feeds into a single convenient feed. FeedBurner also captures and displays useful site analytics, like the number of people reading the feed, what readers they are using, and so on.

feed reader: See *aggregator*.

flogs: A fake blog designed to deceive consumers and others by simulating a situation or story favorable to a company.

A flog, which maliciously deceives to promote the company and its products, should not be confused with a parody blog, such as the Fake Steve Jobs blog, which was open about its artifice and intended strictly for entertainment purposes.

folksonomy: The collective indexing by use of tags, labels, or keywords by the consumers of the content. The tagging system of Flickr or Delicious are examples of folksonomy, which can also be referred to as social indexing.

G

Google Docs: Google's online word processing, spreadsheet, and presentation programs.

H

hat tip: A hat tip is a public acknowledgment to someone for bringing something of interest to the blogger's attention. Also known as H/T or even TOH, Tip Of (the) Hat

hits: A measurement used in web analytics. A hit is defined as any request for a specific file (not a page) from a web server.

HTML: The acronym for Hypertext Markup Language, the coding language used to create and link together documents and files on the web. The code is embedded in and around text and multimedia files in order to define layout, font, colors, and graphics.

hyperlink: Also called simply a link, a navigational reference to another document or page on the web.

I

instant messaging/chat/text messaging/chat rooms: Instant messaging tools support instant communication between two or more people. Some chat tools support audio and video as well. A chat room is an environment in which one or more individuals can communicate with each other.

J

JavaScript: A highly popular scripting language (similar to a programming language) used by website developers. JavaScript is one of the key technology enablers of Web 2.0.

K

keywords: Descriptive words that summarize the contents of a piece of media for the purpose of making it more visible to search engines. Website designers use keywords in the background of the site (unreadable to the user) so that when someone types a certain word or phrase into a search engine, the search engine will find the website. This process of inserting the right keywords, tags, and so on is known as search engine optimization (SEO), which is intended to improve the search engine ranking of a particular page or site.

L

library: Where media assets are stored, organized, and served. Analogy: Similar to a school or public library, online libraries provide the storage, organization, and search and display tools for media. Many times online libraries are called galleries and include photo, audio, and video assets.

link baiting: Link baiting is the act of engaging in controversial conversation or running a promotion that is intended to generate links to the site. Some of these are as blatant as offers of a cash reward randomly given to anyone who links to a particular site during a particular period of time.

Principally, people are bothered by link baiting because the number of links to a site is a key metric affecting where that site will be placed in search results, and therefore the link baiting strategy is generally intended not to make the site more interesting or relevant but to deceive Internet search engines and increase advertising revenue on sites that feature advertising.

Link baiting is perhaps one of the grayer areas of social media ethics, and some would argue that it is not unethical at all.

M

mashup: The term refers to a new breed of web-based applications created by hackers and programmers (often on a volunteer or "hobby" basis) to mix at least two different services from disparate, and even competing, websites. A mashup, for example, could overlay traffic data from one source on the Internet over maps from Yahoo, Microsoft, Google, or any content provider. The term *mashup* comes from the hip-hop music practice of mixing two or more songs. This capability to mix and match data and applications from multiple sources into one dynamic entity is considered by many to represent one of the most important promises of Web 2.0.

meme: A piece of multimedia content, a phrase or even a form of behavior that spreads virally through the Internet.

microblogging: A form of blogging allowing users to publish brief text updates. These messages can be submitted and received by a variety of means and devices, including text messaging, instant messaging, email, mobile device, MP3, or the web. Twitter is an example of a microblogging platform.

milblog: A blog published by active military personnel.

moblogs: Mobile blog. A blog published directly to the web from a phone or other mobile device.

Movable Type: Movable Type is a blog publishing platform created by Six-Apart, the same company that operates TypePad.

MyBlogLog: A Yahoo-owned community and social networking site that tracks traffic and visits to blog content.

MySpace: A social networking site with as many as 100 million users that consists of a network of members' profiles, web logs, photos, email, forums, groups, and more. MySpace was founded in August 2003 by the Internet company eUniverse. In 2006, News Corp bought Intermix Media, parent company of MySpace, for $580 million.

N

navigation (nav): A menu of links or buttons allowing users to move from one web page to another within a site. The menu navigation list is oftentimes listed in the header or footer of a website.

news aggregator: See *aggregator*.

NewsGator: A company that provides a number of RSS aggregators, including FeedDemon, NetNewsWire, and its own web-based feed reader.

Newsvine: An open source, community news service, which lets members customize the news viewed by "seeding" articles or posting for others to view and rate.

NoFollow: An HTML attribute instructing search engines not to allow a hyperlink to a web page to be influenced in ranking by that link. This was originally implemented to combat certain types of search-engine spam.

O

OpenID: A shared identity service that enables users to sign into multiple social networks and social media sites using a single login ID and password. OpenID is a free and open standard under which users are able to control the amount of personal information they provide on websites, and in particular social networking sites. Some of the online and Internet services supporting OpenID include AOL, Blogger, Flickr, LiveDoor, LiveJournal, Vox, Yahoo, WordPress, and others.

open profile: When referring to social networking sites, the term *open profile* describes a dynamic user profile that can be openly shared on (or exported to) other sites where the user is a member. Social networking sites that support open profiles enable users to update their profiles on one site and have those changes automatically reflected on partnering sites.

OpenSocial: Developed by Google Inc., OpenSocial is a set of common APIs for building social applications across multiple websites, including social networking sites. Some websites currently using OpenSocial include LinkedIn, MySpace, and Salesforce.com.

open source: A licensing method that allows others to freely modify programs provided the modifications are made available to the community. The Linux operating system uses an open source license. This form of licensing encourages others to add more value to the product or service.

P

pay per post: Under a pay per post arrangement, a blogger is paid a flat rate per post to publish favorable posts about a company's products and services. Drawing its name from payperpost.com, pay per post is another form of blogola. Pay per post creates confusion among readers as they are generally unaware that the blog they are reading is essentially sponsored by a company that might seem to be receiving objective coverage on the blog.

permalink: Short for permanent link, a permalink is a direct link to a single entry on a blog. As a blog is updated with a new post, that specific post will get its own page with its own URL that can be used to reference and access the page directly, rather than linking to the main URL of the blog. On many blogs the text "permalink" will appear below a blog post as a hyperlink that takes users to the post's own page.

The primary link to your blog might be something like http://blogs.company.com. The permalink, on the other hand, is a permanent link to a particular blog post, and it might look like http://blogs.company.com/09-09-innovation. Many people make the mistake of directing others to their main blog URLs when they intend to direct them to a particular post. You should always use the permalink for this purpose. It can usually be seen by clicking the title of the post, or there may be a link marked "permalink" somewhere on the post.

ping: The term *ping* is borrowed from networking, but it means something slightly different in the world of blogs. A ping occurs when you publish a blog post and your blogging software notifies external websites that your blog has been updated. These in turn notify other sites and services so that your new content is propagated to multiple destinations, such as blog search engines, across the web. Your blog should at the very least ping Google and Technorati. There are also services such as Pingomatic, which ping multiple sites. Do not attempt to ping too often, as this may result in your blog being banned from some search engines and sites.

platform: A platform is the software and technology that provide the foundation upon which a larger application is built. Facebook, for example, has its own platform to allow developers to create new Facebook applications quickly and easily, with the assurance that they will function properly within the Facebook environment. The platform may include the operating system, the development environment, and the protocols for accessing/sharing data and functionality from other programs that reside on the platform.

plug-in: A hardware or software module that adds a specific feature or service to a larger system. The idea of a plug-in is that the new component simply plugs in to the existing system. For example, there are number of plug-ins for Firefox that add functions and capabilities that are not part of the basic browser itself.

podcasting: The recording and online delivery of regularly scheduled audio programming, which can be played back on a computer or an MP3-compatible audio device such as an iPod. Users can subscribe to podcasts to automatically receive updated content when it is published. Podcasting has grown to be as diverse as blogging, with authors, musicians, and professionals across a whole host of industries creating and consuming the content.

post: The text you publish on your blog is called a post. These contain your content and are generally identified by date, time, and sometimes topic.

R

Rich Internet Application (RIA): Web-based applications that require web browsers (or clients) for access. Unlike traditional applications, software installation is not required. However, depending on the application, you usually will need to have ActiveX, Java, Flash, Adobe AIR, or similar technologies (usually available online free of charge) installed on the client machine.

RSS: RSS (really simple syndication) is an XML-based format, and although it can be used in different ways for content distribution, its most widespread usage is in distributing news headlines and updated blog content on the web. Most blogs are equipped with an RSS feed that allows users to subscribe to regular updates from your blog. Whenever your blog is updated, your RSS feed is updated as well. It will generally function in a way that is invisible to you.

S

SaaS: An abbreviation for software as a service. SaaS is a software delivery method that provides access to software and its functions remotely as a web-based service. SaaS allows organizations to access business functionality at a lower cost than paying for licensed applications since SaaS pricing is based on a monthly or transactional fee basis. Also, because the software is hosted remotely, users don't need to invest in additional hardware. SaaS removes the need for organizations to handle installation, setup, daily upkeep, and maintenance. Software as a service may also be referred to as hosted applications.

screen scraping: Screen scraping is the use of technology to "scrape" content from a blog or website and to republish it on another site without permission. Scraping may violate trademark and copyright protections, and it is also specifically banned by many websites and social networks. Screen scraping is so named because instead of using the data output by a program or output from an RSS feed, screen scraping copies, pixel-by-pixel, the information as displayed on the screen.

Second Life : A 3D virtual world where residents create their own images, avatars, and real estate.

SEO: Acronym for search engine optimization, the process of manipulating keywords, links, tags, and so on, to make web content more visible to search engines.

semantic web: An extension of the current web that provides an easier way to find, share, reuse, and combine information by helping machines and databases understand the human language. The semantic web refers to common languages for recording how the data relates to real world objects, allowing a person or a machine to make connections between data through context and meaning.

sidebar: A column along one or both sides of a blog's main content area. The sidebar often includes contact information for the author, the blog's purpose, categories, links to archives, honors, links to feeds, and other items.

social bookmarks: A way for people to store, search, organize, and most importantly, share, web pages they bookmark within web browsers. Two favorites are Delicious and StumbleUpon.

social graph: A social graph is a means of visually representing all of the networks a person belongs to, and the connections between those networks. A social graph is useful for understanding the complex interrelationships between people and their networking behavior, as well as aiding in an understanding of the geometric effect on the size and influence of a person's network that come with belonging to multiple networks.

social network: A social structure made of connections/nodes that are generally individuals or organizations. A social network represents relationships and information flows between people, groups, organizations, animals, computers, or other information/knowledge processing entities. The term itself was coined in 1954 by J. A. Barnes. Can also be the same as a social network site.

social networking site: A social networking site enables users to form relationships within a community of a website. The term can be used to describe community-based websites, online discussion forums, chat rooms, and other social spaces online. Facebook and MySpace are both considered social networks. Can be the same as a social network.

social software: A type of software or web service, generally built on Web 2.0 technology, that allows people to communicate and collaborate while using the application. Software for blogs, wikis, communities, forums, and even instant messaging are all examples of social software.

spambot: Automatic software robots that post spam on blogs and forums.

spider: Automatic software that "wanders" the web, keeping cached copies of web pages for use by search engines. Also called crawlers.

splog: A *splog*, or spam blog, is a spurious blog set up to capture search engine results and divert them to other blogs or websites. The articles are bogus, sometimes using nonsensical text and other times using text specially developed to improve search engine rankings.

stream: The process of transferring data steadily and continuously. Streaming an audio or video file is the process of playing and watching or listening to the file. During streaming, the local computer is not storing the information for any longer than it takes for the user to view or listen to it. Streaming has become the preferred method of multimedia consumption because many users lack the connection speed and computer capacity to frequently download large files. YouTube and other video services like it are primarily streaming video services. Streaming is also useful when the content owner wants to prevent others from downloading their content.

style sheet: Based on CSS (Cascading Style Sheets), a style sheet is comprised of rules that determine the look and feel of a site and define things like fonts, colors, and formatting.

syndication: Enables digital content like a blog to be distributed online via email or RSS reader.

T

tag cloud: A visual representation of frequently used words within a written piece of content. The most popular topics are normally highlighted in a larger, bolder font. Visitors to a blog or site using a tag cloud are able to easily see the most popular tags within the page—making it easy to discern the frequency in which topics are covered in one quick look. Also called a weighted list.

tagging: Web publishers often attach keyword descriptions (called tags or meta tags) to identify images or text within their content. Digital content with matching tags can then be linked together, allowing users to search for similar or related content. If the tags are made public, search engines are able to index them. Tags come in the form of words, acronyms, or numbers.

tags and keywords: Tags and keywords should be attached to every blog (this is done at the implementation level) and to every blog post (which is done during editing and is the responsibility of the blogger.) Keywords and meta tags are the terms that regular search engines, such as Google and Yahoo, use to find a page. Those at the top level—for example, those embedded in the blog home page—should refer to the blog and the company in general terms.

Tags and keywords associated with the post should be specific to that post, and the words or phrases used should be repeated one or more times in the body of the post. In addition to regular HTML tags, you should add Technorati tags with every post.

Technorati: An online database that indexes and searches blogs. Technorati tracks blogs and other forms of social media, including video blogs (vlogs) and podcasts in real time. All this activity is monitored and indexed within minutes of posting of the original content.

thread: A related line of conversation. A thread is a series of entries on a blog, forum, or discussion environment that are related. Some social media have user interfaces designed to allow users to identify and follow specific threads of interest.

trackback: A trackback is similar to a comment, except it is automatically generated. A trackback occurs whenever someone links to your blog from his or her blog. A trackback is similar in appearance to a comment, but it is usually bracketed with [...].

V

viral: Usually an image, article, or video that spreads quickly from person to person with the help of the Internet. Viral videos are remarkable and unique enough to cause the viewers to share them with their friends.

Virtual world: An online environment, such as Second Life or Google Lively, that mimics our physical world. The virtual world is one in which a 2D or 3D environment uses data and imagery to represent physical objects.

vlog: (n.) Short for video blog, the term is used to describe a blog that includes or consists of video clips. Typically updated daily (or with regular frequency), vlogs often reflect the personality or cause of the author. (v.) To author a video blog. Other forms: vlogger (a person who video blogs).

W

walled garden: On the Internet, a walled garden refers to a browsing environment that controls the information and websites the user is able to access. This is a popular method used by ISPs in order to confine user navigation to specific areas of the web, whether for the purpose of shielding users from information—such as restricting children's access to pornography—or directing users to paid content that benefits the ISP. America Online is a good example of a walled garden. Schools are increasingly using the walled garden approach in creating browsing environments in their networks. Students have access to only limited websites, and teachers need a password in order to leave the walled garden and browse the Internet in its entirety.

widget: A small, embeddable software program that extends the functionality of a browser, blog, or other environment without the need for technical expertise on behalf of the user. Widgets can display information and invite interaction. Common widget applications include news feeds, image feeds, weather guides, stock market tickers, and calendars.

wiki: A collaborative space on the web comprised of the perpetual and collective work of multiple authors. Some wikis have a controlled list of authorized editors, and others allow anyone to add, edit, or delete content that has been posted to it. A wiki typically has a detailed audit trail allowing anyone to see who has made edits, when they were made, and any discussion that led up to the edits.

The best known of all wikis is Wikipedia. The term *wiki* refers to either the website or the software used to create the site. "Wiki wiki" means quick in Hawaiian. The first wiki was created by Ward Cunningham in 1995.

Significant portions of this glossary reproduced with the kind permission of Richard Kastelein, Expathos.

Index